THE MISEDUCATION OF INTERPRETING THE BIBLE
Understanding the Mount-Up of Error

Copyright © 2024 by JAMES L. PERRY, SR.

All rights reserved. No part of this book may be reproduced or transmitted in any form or by any means without written permission from the author.

ISBN: 979-8-218-40433-8

DEDICATION

This book is dedicated to my Lord and Savior, Jesus Christ, who has rescued me from the penalty of sin and prepared me to be set for the defense of the gospel. I would also like to dedicate this book to my lovely wife, Cynthia, and my three beautiful children, Priscilla, James Jr., and Jonathan, who make my life complete. Lastly, I dedicate this book to my mentor, confidant, and spiritual father, John A. James, also known as Johnny James "The Walking Bible," who has been the most significant influence in my journey with Christ and has taught me the importance of scriptural integrity and dedication to the study of God's word. He inspired me to write this book and many more to come. You will never know how much I miss you and cherish the memories we shared together as the LORD used you to mold me into the man I am today.

TABLE OF CONTENTS

Preface 6
Introduction 7
Chapter 1 SABBATH DEBATE 13
Chapter 2 CHRISTOLOGY DEBATE.. 23
Chapter 3 Eternal Security Debate 33
Chapter 4 Understanding John 20:17 39
Chapter 5 Are There Apostles Today? 43
Chapter 6 WOMEN ROLE IN MINISTRY 53
Chapter 7 A New Heaven and a New Earth 61
Chapter 8 Understanding Isaiah 53:1-5 & Healing Ministry.................. 67
Chapter 9 The Miseducation of ROMANS 10:9 & The Sinner's Prayer 77
Chapter 10 The Necessity of Water Baptism 86
Chapter 11 Holy Spirit Baptism 97
Chapter 12 TOUCH NOT MINE ANOINTED............................. 113
Chapter 13 Was Jesus able to sin or able not to sin?.................... 117
Chapter 14 Trichotomy vs. Dichotomy 123
Chapter 15 Does God Ever Change His Mind?............................ 129
Chapter 16 Eternal Security & Predestination Debate 139
Chapter 17 Trinity Doctrine 150
Chapter 18 New Birth/Salvation Debate 174
Chapter 19 The Prosperity Gospel.. 190
Chapter 20 Commonly Misinterpreted Scriptures........................ 200
Chapter 21 IDEX of Unbiblical Words and Misused Biblical Words.. 212
Index of References 231

PREFACE

The development of this book came from constant struggles of hearing doctrines taught within Christianity that contradicted each other, especially the Biblical view of certain subjects. I realized that after two thousand plus years removed from the canonization of the Bible and many attempts at translation, many errors developed from misunderstanding, translation errors, manipulations of man, organizational biases, and other things that resulted in the "Mount Up of Error." The "Mount Up of Error" is when you measure something to a copy and not the original, which results in significant mismeasurements. My mentor, Dr. Johnny James, introduced this term to me and gave me an illustration due to his experience as a sign painter in Detroit, MI, where he would use yardsticks for his sign painting business. Johnny James explained he wanted to make several yardsticks handy one day. He measured the first one against the original, then the second against the copy instead of the original, and continued in that same process. When completing several of the yardsticks, he realized that the last one he completed was significantly shorter than the original. While working, he did not notice that each yardstick was becoming shorter and shorter because each measurement was only a centimeter off the last copy he measured against. The gradual discrepancy was not noticeable until the end. He said that he learned the lesson then that you are supposed to always measure against the original and not a copy. This mismeasurement is what the "Mount Up of Error" is and the reason for authoring this book.

INTRODUCTION

The purpose of this book is to address the many erroneous teachings and heretical beliefs of professing Christians today. There needs to be an accurate search for truth in the modern movement of Christianity. Many believers in this twenty-first century are shallow in their faith with no regard for pursuing orthodoxy. They are casual, do not see the problem of denominations, and are blind to the fact that the Bible they read does not support their form of worship, making their faith carnal and contemporary to the degree that it is in assimilation to the world and not the Kingdom of God. Many beliefs are according to the traditions of men, organizational dogmas, fanaticism, emotionalism, sensationalism, cultural contexts, and dramatizations of scripture, but there is no real contention for the faith. Colossians 2:8 teaches, "Beware lest any man spoil you through philosophy and vain deceit, after the tradition of men, after the rudiments of the world, and not after Christ (KJV)." Many are content with denominationalism, filled with tolerance and a striving for ecumenicalism but not a burden for truth. This burden for truth does not come from a self-righteous and biased view of specific belief systems but an honest view of scripture. There should not be thousands of denominations or divisions of doctrines but one united church that is united and not fractioned. I firmly believe that the church is supposed to earnestly contend for the faith once delivered unto the saints and for a standard belief system or the same view of salvation that they were united in (Jude 1:3, KJV). We see from the scriptures that doctrines tried to infiltrate the early church. Still, Paul said, "I marvel that ye are so soon removed from him that called you into the grace of Christ unto another gospel: Which is not another; but there be some that trouble you, and would pervert the gospel of Christ (Gal. 1:6-7, KJV)."

The modern church is over two thousand years removed from when it was established in Jerusalem, and from that time, there have been many fractions and separations from the gospel truth. These fractions have caused an extreme "mount-up" of error. There have been attempts in past centuries to bring attention to specific heretical belief systems and doctrines of apostasy, such as the Reformation period. However, the so-called Reformation period had some problems that confused many believers, and many errors evolved. Martin Luther and others such as Ulrich Zwingli were part of this reformation period that separated themselves from the Roman Catholic system. They tried to correct some errors that seemed to damage the faith and the parishioners who adhered to the dogmas and rudiments of the Roman Catholic system. The problem that the reformists had that resulted in even more confusion was they measured themselves up to the Roman Catholic church instead of the church of Jerusalem. The abandonment of first-century theology is called the "Mount Up of Error," when you measure something to a copy, not the original. The effects of this will eventually result in mismeasurements.

I was introduced to this concept by my mentor, Dr. Johnny James, who illustrated this due to his experience as a sign painter in Detroit, MI, where he used yardsticks for his sign painting business. He explained that one day, he wanted to make several yardsticks to have handy. He measured the first one against the original, then the second against the copy instead of the original, and continued in that same process. When he completed several of the yardsticks, he realized that the last one he completed was significantly shorter than the original. As he was working, he could not tell he was making them shorter and shorter because each measurement was not highly noticeable, getting shorter and shorter. The gradual discrepancy was apparent at the end. He said that he learned the lesson then that you are supposed to always measure against the original and not a copy. When you do not measure from the original, that is what the "Mount Up of Error" is. Martin Luther and the many others that came after him, like Ulrich Zwingli, John Calvin, and many more men, turned themselves to a copy instead of measuring themselves to the original, so now there are many professing Christians that have come up short due to the "Mount Up of Error." The "Mount of Error" is why the forms of Christianity that came to America were already tainted with the many pagan rituals and erroneous teachings, and the teachings of the first church established in Jerusalem were absent in many ways. The erroneous teachings have caused many fractions because every effort to correct teachings became another denomination, but they have yet to return to the original, and the error grew exponentially.

This book is not for everybody and would bring debate, but it is critical in understanding Biblical interpretation. However, it is not for those content to rest in traditional and denominational biases but for those who have wondered why we have so many different beliefs of a singular faith. The miseducation of Christians is to aid the believer in getting answers to the many doctrines that divide them and to help them be more vigilant and sober in their faith. This book will also point out the many things said and done in the churches around the world that are not Biblical and do not pertain to the New Testament church.

"My people are destroyed for lack of knowledge: because thou have rejected knowledge, I will also reject thee (Hosea 4:6, KJV). This book's cry is to bring light to ignorance and promote the knowledge of the LORD so Christians will not be miseducated but enlightened by the truth of the LORD. John 8:32 states, "And ye shall know the truth, and the truth shall make you free (KJV)." The only way bondage can exist is if there is a void of knowledge. The lack of sharing knowledge is a tactic used in the history of keeping people in slavery. The enslavers made education illegal for all enslaved people because once a person learns, then their mind craves truth to the point of self-actualization, and then their mind is free. Once a person's mind is free, they will learn how to live free. Hiding knowledge is also why the Roman Catholic church did not allow parishioners to read or have translations of Bibles because if the parishioners read the Bible, they would learn the truth and realize that the Bible did not support the system they were in and would leave the Roman Catholic church. Therefore, this book was written to free the minds of believers in Christ and break down denominational walls so people will have life through their understanding of the word of God and no longer be destroyed for the lack of knowledge! A lot of preachers thrive off the miseducation of the Christian because it is the only way they can support their lifestyle of intemperance and greed. If the people of the LORD ever learn of their shenanigans, they will no longer be able to fill up their mega-churches, live in their million-dollar estates, and fly their million-dollar jets. "Through covetousness shall they with feigned words make merchandise of you (2 Peter 2:3)."

Paul mentions to the Galatians, "I marvel that ye are so soon removed from him that called you into the grace of Christ unto another gospel: 7 Which is not another; but there be some that trouble you, and would pervert the gospel of Christ. 8 But though we, or an angel from heaven, preach any other gospel unto you than that which we have preached unto you, let him be accursed. 9 As we said before, so say I now again, If any man preach any other gospel unto you than that ye have received, let him be accursed (Galatians 1:6 KJV). The word "another" in verse six is the Greek word "ἕτερος (heteros)," which means another of a different kind. Heteros is where the English language borrows from the Greek language to create the word Heterosexual. The term heterosexual is about humans but a diverse kind of the same species. On the other hand, the word "another" in verse seven of Galatians chapter one is the Greek word "ἄλλος," and although "ἄλλος" is translated as "another," the word "ἄλλος" means another of the same kind. In context, there is no other gospel besides the true gospel, and all other so-called gospel is false. There is an absolution to the gospel and no room for multiple interpretations.

I am convinced that this rapid number of erroneous teachings and false doctrines is a plan of the enemy and a sign of the last times. In 2 Thessalonians 2:7, "For the mystery of iniquity doth already work: only he who now letteth will let until he is taken out of the way (KJV)." This "mystery" ("μυστήριον" musterion) is considered the secret plan or secret teaching that was hidden but will be revealed in time. The (musterion) is a hidden teaching of iniquity or what is better translated as lawlessness. The enemy plans to teach lawlessness, and because there is a failure of contending for the faith or being as Paul, "set for the defense of the gospel (Phil. 1:17, KJV)," this lawlessness has allowed corruption to come in among the saints of God. Jude mentions, "For certain men have secretly slipped in among you– men who long ago were marked out for the condemnation I am about to describe– ungodly men who have turned the grace of our God into a license for evil and who deny our only Master and Lord, Jesus Christ (Jud 1:4 NET)." Although this has been happening since the first century, it has become more extensive in propagation because the first century did not deal with it as how the 21st century does. There are more than 45000 Christian denominations globally, and fractions within fractions have an even more staggering number. Timothy describes the last days or times as "some shall depart from the faith, giving heed to seducing spirits, and doctrines of devils (1Ti 4:1 KJV)." However, the church strove to conform to its message in the first century. 1 Corinthian 1:10 states, "Now I beseech you, brethren, by the name of our Lord Jesus Christ, that ye all speak the same thing, and that there be no divisions among you; but that ye be perfectly joined together in the same mind and the same judgment." Suppose a parishioner asks a member of the clergy or their pastor why we teach a specific theology in a particular way that is not consistent with Biblical traditions or concepts. In that case, they will either try to explain it away or say that it has always been taught this way. This answer should not be adequate for any believer in Christ! Some pastors do not allow parishioners to ask questions in Bible study because they do not want to look incompetent. However, this is wrong because the Bible was always studied and understood communally. Only to take instructions without asking questions is a hindrance to the growth and maturity of believers. The Bible teaches in 1 Peter 3:15 to "be ready always to give an answer to every man that asketh you a reason of the hope that is in you with meekness and fear. (KJV)" Every pastor or preacher should always be able to answer the questions of parishioners or anyone who seeks understanding.

CHAPTER 1 SABBATH DEBATE

Miseducation: God requires Sabbath-keeping of the New Testament Church.

Colossians 2:16-17 Therefore do not let anyone judge you by what you eat or drink, or with regard to a religious festival, a New Moon celebration or a Sabbath day. These are a shadow of the things that were to come; the reality, however, is found in Christ (KJV).

Romans 14:5 "One man considers one day more sacred than another; another man considers every day alike. Each one should be fully convinced in his own mind (KJV).

These Scriptures make it clear that, for the Christian, Sabbath-keeping is a matter of spiritual freedom, not a command from God. Sabbath-keeping is an issue on which God's Word instructs us not to judge each other. Sabbath-keeping is a matter about which each Christian needs to be fully convinced in his/her own mind.

In the early chapters of the book of Acts, the first Christians were predominantly Jews. When Gentiles began to receive the gift of salvation through Jesus Christ, the Jewish Christians had a dilemma. What aspects of the Mosaic Law and Jewish tradition should Gentile Christians be instructed to obey? The apostles met and discussed the issue in the Jerusalem council (Acts 15). The decision was, "It is my judgment, therefore, that we should not make it difficult for the Gentiles who are turning to God. Instead, we should write to them, telling them to abstain from food polluted by idols, from sexual immorality, from the meat of strangled animals and from blood" (Acts 15:19-20). Sabbath-keeping was not one of the commands the apostles felt was necessary to force on Gentile believers. It is inconceivable that the apostles would neglect to include Sabbath-keeping if it were God's command for Christians to observe the Sabbath day.

A common error in the Sabbath-keeping debate is the concept that the Sabbath was the day of worship. Groups such as the Seventh Day Adventists hold that God requires the church service to be held on Saturday, the Sabbath day. That is not what the Sabbath command was. The Sabbath command was to do no work on the Sabbath day (Exodus 20:8-11). Nowhere in Scripture is the Sabbath day commanded to be the day of worship. Yes, Jews in the Old Testament, New Testament, and modern times use Saturday as the day of worship, but that is not the essence of the Sabbath command. In the book of Acts, whenever a meeting is said to be on the Sabbath, it is a meeting of Jews, not Christians.

When did the early Christians meet? Acts 2:46-47 gives us the answer, "Every day they continued to meet together in the temple courts. They broke bread in their homes and ate together with glad and sincere hearts, praising God and enjoying the favor of all the people. And the Lord added to their number daily those who were being saved." If there was a day that Christians met regularly, it was the first day of the week (our Sunday), not the Sabbath day (our Saturday) (Acts 20:7; 1 Corinthians 16:2). The myth that Christians began to worship on a pagan day of Sunday because of the Norse meaning of the day, being the Egyptian Sun god day for Ra is ridiculous because if that is the case then those who worship on Saturday is worshiping the Saturn god because that is where Saturday comes from. Contrary to these beliefs, Sunday is actually "Yom rishon," which is the first day of the week, and Old Testament Israel, as well as the New Testament Body of Christ, assembled on the first day quite often. To go even further, it was not until 321 AD that the emperor Constantine officially decreed a seven-day week in the Roman Empire, and then it spread to Europe, and that is how we received the modern names of the weekdays we use currently. This is why Sunday has nothing to do with Christians worshiping on Sunday because, as Acts 20:7 states, "And upon **the first day of the week**, when the disciples came together to break bread, Paul preached unto them, ready to depart on the morrow; and continued his speech until midnight (KJV). There is no mention of a worship day on Saturday as a customary practice or commandment. In honor of Christ's resurrection on Sunday, the early Christians observed Sunday not as the "Christian Sabbath" but as a day to worship Jesus Christ especially. John 20:1 said, "The **first day of the week** cometh Mary Magdalene early, when it was yet dark, unto the sepulchre, and seeth the stone taken away from the sepulchre (KJV).

Is there anything wrong with worshipping on Saturday, the Jewish Sabbath? Absolutely not! We should worship God every day, not just on Saturday or Sunday! Many churches today have both Saturday and

Sunday services. There is freedom in Christ (Romans 8:21; 2 Corinthians 3:17; Galatians 5:1). Should a Christian practice Sabbath-keeping, that is, not working on Saturdays? If a Christian feels led to do so, absolutely, yes (Romans 14:5). However, those who choose to practice Sabbath-keeping should not judge those who do not keep the Sabbath (Colossians 2:16). Further, those who do not keep the Sabbath should avoid being a stumbling block (1 Corinthians 8:9) to those who do keep the Sabbath. Galatians 5:13-15 summarizes the whole issue: "You, my brothers, were called to be free. But do not use your freedom to indulge the sinful nature; rather, serve one another in love. The entire law is summed up in a single command: 'Love your neighbor as yourself.' If you keep on biting and devouring each other, watch out or you will be destroyed by each other."

Let us examine some of the commandments from the LORD concerning keeping the Sabbath:

"Everyone is to stay where he is on the seventh day; no one is to go out" (Exodus 16:29).

How many Sabbatarians break the Sabbath every week by traveling, even going to "worship" God on the Sabbath?

"Do not light a fire in any of your dwellings on the Sabbath day" (Exodus 35:3).

How many Sabbatarians break the Sabbath by lighting a fire in their houses on the Sabbath to cook to keep warm or just to sit in front of a cozy fireplace?

"Whoever does any work on it [the Sabbath] must be put to death" (Exodus 35:2).

A man was found gathering wood on a Sabbath day. "The Lord said to Moses, 'The man must die. The whole assembly must stone him outside the camp.' So, the assembly took him outside the camp and stoned him to death, as the Lord commanded Moses" (Numbers 15:32-36). How many Sabbatarians obey God by the whole assembly, taking a man out and stoning him to death for even gathering wood for a fire on the Sabbath?

We must compare scripture with scripture to arrive at truth, doctrine, and practice under the new and better Covenant. Notwithstanding the fact that God, as recorded in Genesis by Moses after the days of Abraham, Isaac, and Jacob (Israel), rested (ceased from His work) and blessed the seventh day and made it holy, it was a shadow or type of the Sabbath to come, which is Jesus Christ himself.

True Christians, whether born-again Jews or Gentiles, have entered the Sabbath Rest, Jesus Christ. Jesus himself did not keep the Sabbath. On the Sabbath, "Jesus said to them [the Jews], 'My Father is always at His work to this very day, and I, too, am working.' For this reason, the Jews tried all the harder to kill Him; not only was He breaking the Sabbath, but He was even calling God His own Father, making himself equal with God" (John 5:17-18). Some of the Pharisees said, "This man is not from God, for He does not keep the Sabbath" (John 9:16).

Jesus did not sin by not keeping the Sabbath because He was, and is, sinless. Indeed, Jesus is The Sabbath, where Christians (saved Jews and Gentiles) rest. All those who have not been born again, whether Jews or Gentiles, have not entered The Sabbath rest. Unsaved Jews are still under the Mosaic Law and must keep the Sabbath, as well as the rest of the Law, and if they break the Law at just one point, they are guilty of breaking the whole Law.

Speaking of the Sabbath given to the Israelites (Jews), the writer to the Hebrews said, "For if Joshua had given them rest, God would not have spoken later about another day. There remains, then, a Sabbath rest for the people of God [born-again Jews and Gentiles]; for anyone who enters God's rest also rests from his own work, just as God did from His" (Hebrews 4:8-10). Jesus said, "Come unto me all you who are weary and heavy laden, and I will give you rest."

Concerning the Sabbath, the Law says, "Everyone is to stay where he is on the seventh day; no one is to go out" (Exodus 16:29), but the apostle Paul and those Christians with him went contrary to the Law as revealed in this one passage alone, "On the Sabbath we went outside the city gate to the river..." (Acts 16:13). Paul and those Christians with him were not sinning by not keeping the Sabbath. The great apostle knew that Jesus had taught him by the Holy Spirit that the Old Covenant sabbaths were a shadow and type of the coming Messiah and Savior, who is The Sabbath. It is only in Him that we can truly find rest for our souls that have been laden with sin.

There was a period of transition for a sizable number of years between Judaism under the Old Covenant and Christianity under the New. The Jews who repented of their sins and received Christ as their Savior and Christ as their Sabbath Rest would not readily let go of their Jewish traditions. But when the apostle Paul was raised up, the Lord taught Jews and Gentiles more things that were not revealed during Jesus' earthly ministry. Paul said, "One man considers one day more sacred than another; another man considers every day alike. Each one should be fully convinced in his own mind. He who regards one day as special, does so to the Lord...Therefore let us stop passing judgment on one another...So whatever you believe about these things keep between yourself and God" (Romans 14:5-6, 13, 22).

When the Jewish Christians saw that God was granting repentance to the Gentiles, the leaders did not know what to require of them. So, they met and decided not to tell them to keep the Sabbath, but rather to "abstain from food sacrificed to idols, from blood, from meat of strangled animals, and from sexual immorality" (Acts 15:12-29). This took place at the Council of Jerusalem in A.D. 50.

The early Christians met in houses on the Lord's Day which is the first day of the week. The Sabbath, which is the seventh day of the week, is still the Sabbath. The Sabbath has not been changed to the first day of the week, as some claim. The Roman Catholics did not institute worship on the Lord's Day, contrary to their false claims. This is a deception not only taught by Roman Catholic theologians, but by others such as the Seventh Day Adventists (and similar cults). The Seventh Day Adventists and some other Sabbatarians are so deceived and so hung up on the Sabbath (which none really keep) that they go to the absurd extreme of claiming that worshipping on the Lord's Day is taking the mark of the beast! Much more could be said about the subject, but more than enough has been revealed for the Holy Spirit to confirm to those who have "ears to hear" that what has been presented here is, indeed, true.

Old vs. New Testament/Covenant Commands

Furthermore, the Sabbath law was given to Israel. The Old Covenant was to the nation of Israel and not to the Gentiles (Acts 15).

> *Ezekiel 20:10-12 Wherefore I caused them to go forth out of the land of Egypt, and brought them into the wilderness. 11 And I gave them my statutes, and shewed them my judgments, which if a man do, he shall even live in them. 12 Moreover also **I gave them my sabbaths**, to be a sign between me and them, that they might know that I am the Lord that sanctify them. (KJV)*

GOD gave Israel his Sabbath as a sign of his covenant to them, and it was actually plural, "Sabbaths." The so-called Sabbath keepers today try to recognize the Sabbath day but there were also Sabbath weeks and years that they were to keep as a commandment. However, the emphasis is that the Sabbath was between GOD and Israel. The New Testament church only must obey the Old Testament laws if it was reinstituted and reiterated in the New Testament writings. When JESUS spoke to the man in Matthew chapter 19, the man replied asked "what good thing shall I do, that I may have eternal life? And he (JESUS) said unto him, Why callest thou me good? there is none good but one, that is, God: but if thou wilt enter into life, keep the commandments. He saith unto him, Which? Jesus said, Thou shalt do no murder, Thou shalt not commit adultery, Thou shalt not steal, Thou shalt not bear false witness, Honour thy father and thy mother: and, Thou shalt love thy neighbour as thyself. The young man saith unto him, All these things have I kept from my youth up: what lack I yet (KJV)?" Notice, JESUS did not mention the Sabbath.

GOD always establish a sign of a covenant with his people just as he gave Noah the Rainbow as a sign of the covenant that he will not flood the earth again, he gave Abraham the circumcision as a sign of his covenant that GOD will fulfil his promise of making a great nation of out him, he gave Israel his Sabbaths as a sign between Israel and himself and to the New Covenant church he gave the Holy Spirit as a sign of the New Testament covenant. The Body of Christ is not Israel and is in a new covenant with GOD. A new covenant is an amendment to the Old Testament and just like any legal document or living will, if the testator or person who creates the legal document decides to create a codicil or amendment then no matter what was in the previous will it becomes null and void. In this case "JESUS, the testator and mediator of the New Covenant according to Heb. 9:16,17 and 12:24, KJV)," and the activator of how GOD wants to continue a relationship with his people and all testators have an executioner of their will and the church is the executioner and that is why the church needs to avoid erroneous teachings. The important thing to understand is that the Sabbath laws were not only to Israel, but it was an Old Testament commandment and James 2:10 states, "For whosoever shall keep the whole law, and yet offend in one point, he is guilty of all (KJV)." This scripture by itself has indicted the modern-day Sabbath keepers because they are trying to keep the Sabbath and breaking the Sabbath by violating its ordinances. This means according to James 2:10 that they should receive the punishment of breaking all of the commandments by offending in one part of it.

CHAPTER 2 CHRISTOLOGY DEBATE

Miseducation: God is Jehovah/Yahweh Sr., and Jesus is Jehovah/Yahweh Jr.

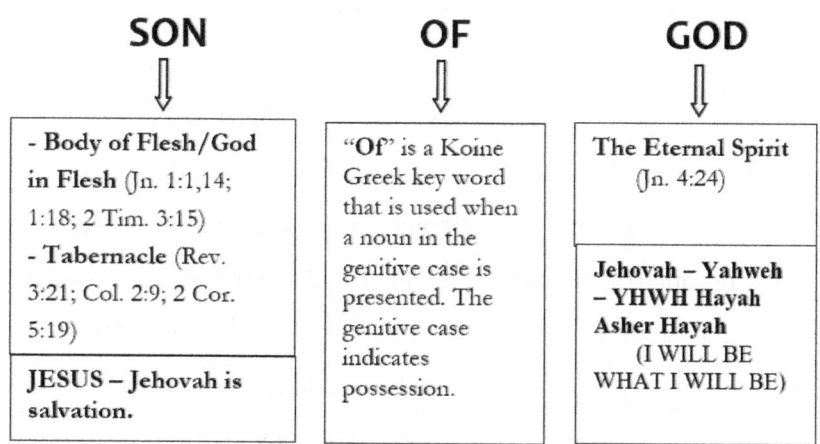

I came across a paper that a brother in Christ wrote about the term "Son of God." In this document, the brother concluded that God is Jesus' senior, and the Son is Jesus' junior. For this purpose, this is an address to explain how the understanding of the term "Son of God" cannot be understood as "Son" to be Jesus Junior and "God" to be Jesus Senior. This is a dangerous doctrine that could lead to much confusion and destroy orthodoxy as it brings strength to the pagan theology of Jesus being no more than a demi-god or a delegate. There has been much confusion over time about the body of Jesus or the flesh of Jesus, which has caused many teachings to spring up since the first century until now. Therefore, this thesis will discuss the name of

Jesus, the flesh of Jesus, the word manifest, the Greek keyword "of," and the term Son of God.

The Name of Jesus and of God

I would like to explain the onomatology of the name of Jesus. Jesus in Greek is (Ἰησοῦς Iesous), and in Hebrew, it is (יְהוֹשֻׁעַ Yehowshuwa`), and the meaning of both whether in Greek and Hebrew declares that Jehovah is salvation. Therefore, in Matthew 1:23, it was proclaimed that Jesus would be "Emmanuel, which being interpreted is, God with us (KJV)." The history of God's usage of names in the Old Testament is significant to the coming of our LORD. Throughout the history of Israel, the Jewish people would always attach a description to God's name based on his performance, which built his great reputation. When he provided, they called him Jehovah Jireh (Gen. 22:14); when he healed, they called him Jehovah rophe (Ex. 15:26); when he gave peace, they called him Jehovah Shalom (Jud. 6:24); when he fought their battles, they called him Jehovah nissi (Ex. 17:15), and when it was time to bring salvation for the penalty of sin, we now call him Jehovah is salvation (JESUS)! Not Jesus Junior but the only one that can save, heal, give peace, provide, and fight battles is Jehovah the ALMIGHTY GOD! When Jesus states, "I am come in my Father's name, and ye receive me not: if another shall come in his own name, him ye will receive (Joh 5:43 KJV)," he is not making a declaration that he is Jesus Junior or a representative of Jesus Senior but that name belongs to him because in Matthew 24:5 he declares that many will try to come in his name. Jesus is God's consummated name, for listening to the words of Paul in Philippians 2:9-11 states,

"Wherefore God also hath highly exalted him, and given him a name which is above every name: That at the name of Jesus every knee should bow, of things in heaven, and things in earth, and things under the earth; And that every tongue should confess that Jesus Christ is Lord, to the glory of God the Father (KJV)." If every knee should bow and every tongue confesses to Jesus that he is Lord, then if God is Jesus' senior, that leaves him without any worship because all the admiration will go to Jesus Junior. However, this is not true. This declaration by the apostle Paul only echoes the prophetic utterance of Zechariah in 14:9, which states, "And the LORD shall be king over all the earth: in that day shall there be one LORD, and his name one (KJV)." This is an eschatological scripture and will be explained further in-depth later in this thesis.

The Flesh of Jesus

The Flesh or Body that Jesus walked around in should not be confused with a demi-god, a second person in the Godhead, or Jesus Junior. We first must understand what gives a body or flesh life. A body does not represent a person but is merely a covering or vehicle for that person. In Genesis 2:7, "the LORD God formed man of the dust of the ground and breathed into his nostrils the breath of life; and man became a living soul (KJV)." Without the breath (נְשָׁמָה neshamah) of God, the body that God formed would have been just an empty carcass. So, we must understand that the body that walked on earth and did wonders as the "Son of God" was not Jesus, but it was Jesus' tabernacle according to Revelation 21:3. This body had the Spirit of God without measure, according to John 3:34. This is what gave life to the body that God created to redeem the world as the Lamb of God. God did not send a representative; he came himself and supplied a vehicle for him to travel in. Since God is a spirit, "No man hath seen God at any time; the only begotten Son, which is in the bosom of the Father, he hath declared him (Joh 1:18 KJV)." God, being a spirit, needed a body to use on earth. The term "the only begotten Son" is tricky because in most Greek manuscripts, there is no word in this text that can be translated into "Son." Son comes from the Greek word (υἱός huios), and in this text, it is not there, but rather, the Greek word (θεός theos) is used. So, the term should read "the only begotten God." "Only begotten" is the Greek word (μονογενής monogenes). This word has two parts, including mono and genes. Mono means only or one, and genes means nature, and where the English language borrows from the use of genetics or genes. This means Jesus was the "monogenes Theos," one of the exact nature of God. He also declares God because declare is the same Greek word expositors like to use in explaining the word of God, which is exegesis (ἐξηγέομαι exegeomai). This means since no man has ever seen God because he is a spirit, then, Jesus became the exegesis of God and put a face on God or gave the eternal spirit a body to work in. Not as Jesus Junior but as the Almighty God, an eternal spirit who came to us in bodily form. Therefore, Colossians 2:9 states, "For in him dwelleth all the fulness of the Godhead bodily (KJV)." I must point out that the term "Godhead" is the Greek word (θεότης theotes), which is properly defined as "deity," and so all the deity or God was dwelling in a body and used as the Messiah or the Son of God. I would be remiss if I did not give the understanding that the term "Son" can also be translated from (υἱός huios) as "descendant" as well. The God that was in glory descended on earth as the Messiah.

God was Manifested

The word manifest, used in many scriptures to describe the phenomenon of God appearing in the flesh, is easily understood when the word is taken from its first use and origins. The Greek word (φανερόω phaneroo) means to make manifest or visible or known what has been hidden or unknown, to manifest, whether by words, or deeds or in any other way 1a) make actual and visible, realized. Also, to expose to view, make manifest, to show oneself, appear, to become known, to be plainly recognized, thoroughly understood who and what one is. With this definition we cannot confuse who Jesus the "Son of God" is. 1 Timothy 3:16 says, "And without controversy great is the mystery of godliness: God was manifest in the flesh, justified in the Spirit, seen of angels, preached unto the Gentiles, believed on in the world, received up into glory (KJV)." This means God appeared or the eternal spirit became visible in the flesh. In John 1:14 there is a word used that declares that the WORD OF GOD in John 1:1 "became or was made flesh" and this word is (γίνομαι ginomai). This word has the same meaning as manifest in 1 Timothy 3:16. The same way Jesus is God manifest in the flesh in 1 Tim. 3:16 and the WORD of God that became flesh in John 1:1,14 is the same way he is "the grace of God that bringeth salvation hath appeared to all men (Tit 2:11 KJV)." The word appeared is the Greek word (ἐπιφαίνω epiphaino), and it also means to appear or become visible. For this reason, Jesus is not another god, demi-god, the second person in a tri-unity, or even Jesus Junior. He is simply the

Eternal God that appeared, became visible, or made himself known unto sinners to bring great salvation. It is true that God got into the flesh, but without God getting into the flesh, that flesh would have been just an empty carcass without any life at all. God prepared himself a body that was "holy, harmless, undefiled, separate from sinners, and made higher than the heavens (Heb 7:26 KJV)" and got in it. Notice the word made, which is (γίνομαι ginomai)." God got into the greatest thing he ever made so he could do the greatest thing he ever did, which is bring a GREAT SALVATION! To wit, that God was in Christ, reconciling the world unto himself, not imputing their trespasses unto them; and hath committed unto us the word of reconciliation (2Co 5:19 KJV)."

The Greek Key Word "OF"

The genitive case can indicate possession. It uses genitive case endings, and its keywords are "of and from." So, in the case of the term "Son of God," there are a few ways we can understand it. First, if we look at this in the literal understanding of Greek grammar, then the word in the genitive usually follows the word it is modifying (υἱὸς τοῦ θεοῦ). To the novice reader, it would look as if God possessed the "Son." This sounds like it could be right since we know God was in Christ, but since the terms "Son of God" and "Son of Man" are used interchangeably, then that would also mean that man possesses the "Son" or has ownership of the "Son." This cannot be true because he did not have the nature of man in him. After all, that would have caused him to have the Adamic nature, which would have flawed the Lamb of God; let us look at this in another way. Since "Son" is the head noun and the subject of every text it is in, then it is more plausible to understand it as the "Son" possesses "God." Not as the Son is in God, but the "Son" possesses qualities of God or possesses the nature of "God." Only then can it be used interchangeably with the "Son of Man" because he also possessed qualities as a man because he "was made in the likeness of men: And being found in fashion as a man (Phi 2:7,8 KJG)." Context is especially important when reading scripture so that we do not err when reading it. Ephesians chapter 6, verses 13-17, has several statements that use the same genitive rule, such as the breastplate of righteousness, the gospel of peace, the shield of faith, the helmet of salvation, and the sword of the spirit. For example, faith does not possess the shield, but faith is your shield, and salvation does not possess the helmet, but salvation is your helmet, so neither does God possess the Son, but God is the Son, and the Son is God.

Son of God on Earth and in Glory

If Jesus is the "Son of God" throughout his earthly ministry, we must recognize his status in glory as well. When John uses the term "Son of God" in the book of Revelation, he states, "And unto the angel of the church in Thyatira write, These things saith the Son of God, who hath his eyes like unto a flame of fire, and his feet are like fine brass (Rev. 2:18 KJV)." This same "Son of God" in glory is proclaimed in Revelation 1:11 as the "Alpha and Omega, the first and the last (KJV)." Now, if Jesus the "Son of God" is Jesus Junior, then how could he be proclaimed as the "Alpha" and the "First?" If he is only a Junior, he should have excluded those terms and simply called himself "Omega" and "Last." However, he is called the "Son of God" in Rev. 2:18 because this part of scripture discusses a time before the consummation of the end times, and Jesus is still operating in his messianic role. When the end comes, and he no longer needs to operate in his messianic role, then the consummation will take place, and "The LORD will then be king over all the earth. In that day, the LORD will be seen as one with a single name (Zec 14:9 NET)." Not a Jesus Senior and a Jesus Junior, one name which has been all the time throughout eternity. If God declares he will be king in glory in Zechariah 14:9 and Jesus is declared to be King of Kings in Revelation 19:16, then will there be a power struggle between Jesus Senior and Jesus Junior? ABSOLUTELY NO! They are both the same, and there will only be one king because we all will be able to behold this eternal spirit that we call God. After all, the eternal spirit will give us eternal eyes to behold the eternal spirit in his eternal image, which will be the eternal Jesus! The "Son of God" is not Jesus Junior, according to 1 John 5:20, but is the "true God."

Son of God in Prophesy

Another point we need to understand about the term "Son of God" is that it derives from Old Testament prophesy. The Hebrew understanding of the term "Son of God" is that it is delegated to a messianic understanding. In Daniel 7:13 it says, "I saw in the night visions, and behold, one like the Son of man came with the clouds of heaven, and came to the Ancient of days, and they brought him near before him (KJV)." This is pointing to the Messiah conquering at the end of the ages and is also referenced to Jesus in the New Testament in Mark 13:26 as "the Son of man coming in the clouds with great power and glory (KJV)." The Jewish people always understood the prophesy of the Messiah as the Son of Man. Son of Man was used instead of Son of God because of the sensitivity and commandment to not use the Lord thy God in vain. So, the unutterable name could not be used. Only in Daniel 3:25 was the Son of God used, but it was used in a pagan understanding that the pagan Chaldeans saw a fourth person in the fiery furnace that looked like a son of a god, but we must note that since the Jewish scribe included this Biblical account, then they understood it as the Mighty God that manifested his power to the witness of man. This was a messianic vision and prophetic utterance of the Old Testament, alluding to the messiah. In the New Testament, the Son of Man and the Son of God were used interchangeably depending on who the audience was. If it was a strict Pharisee audience, then Son of Man was used, and if it was Gentile, Samaritan, or any group that was not legalistic, then Son of God was used.

CHAPTER 3 ETERNAL SECURITY DEBATE

Miseducation: *The term **"once save always saved"** has a meaning of once you have been born again then it is impossible to fall from grace because the work that Jesus did on the cross secured all those that come to him for salvation.*

This teaching gives professing Christians a false sense of hope that no matter what they do or how they live they will be saved from the wrath to come. They have been lured into a loose lifestyle of degradation and reproach. The term to describe this error is antinomianism. This is defined as one who holds that under the gospel dispensation of grace, the moral law is of no use or obligation because faith alone is necessary for salvation. This is more widely known as the doctrine of eternal security which is a reformed doctrine whose champion is John Calvin. This doctrine holds to the sort of perseverance of the saints, according to which true Christians will persevere in good works and faith because faith is God's perfect gift, and it will inevitably produce salvation not requiring a life of holiness or Biblical morality. One of the main scriptures that are used to support this doctrine is Romans 5:20, which states, "Moreover the law entered, that the offence might abound. But where sin abounded, grace did much more abound (KJV)." I have heard the miseducation and error of this text by the adherents of the doctrine to make the text be used as a license to sin. I heard a preacher say that no matter how much I sin grace will rise above that sin to keep him eternally secure in Christ. It is true that the LORD has grace, and according to 1 John 1:9 "If we confess our sins, he is faithful and just to forgive us our sins, and to cleanse us from all unrighteousness (KJV)." But this is not a license to sin because Paul instructs the Roman church, saying:

What shall we say then? Shall we continue in sin, that grace may abound? 2 God forbid. How shall we, that are dead to sin, live any longer therein (Rom 6:1-2)?

A question we must ask ourselves is, if we are eternally secured and nothing we do can put us out of the will of God, then to believe this it will take ignoring too many scriptures such as:

1 Timothy 4:1 Now the Spirit speaketh expressly, that in the latter times some shall depart from the faith, giving heed to seducing spirits, and doctrines of devils; (KJV)

2 Thessalonians 2:3 Let no man deceive you by any means: for that day shall not come, except there come a falling away first, and that man of sin be revealed, the son of perdition; (KJV)

2 Peter 3:17 Ye therefore, beloved, seeing ye know these things before, beware lest ye also, being led away with the error of the wicked, fall from your own stedfastness. (KJV)

2 Timothy 4:3-4 For the time will come when they will not endure sound doctrine; but after their own lusts shall they heap to themselves teachers, having itching ears; 4 And they shall turn away their ears from the truth, and shall be turned unto fables. (KJV)

Galatians 5:4 You who are trying to be declared righteous by the law have been alienated from Christ; you have fallen away from grace! (NET)

2 Peter 2:20-21 For if after they have escaped the pollutions of the world through the knowledge of the Lord and Saviour Jesus Christ, they are again entangled therein, and overcome, the latter end is worse with them than the beginning. 21 For it had been better for them not to have known the way of righteousness, than, after they have known it, to turn from the holy commandment delivered unto them. (KJV)

There are many more scriptures that discuss the possibility of apostasy from the LORD. These scriptures cannot be ignored, or they can be overlooked because one or two seem to say something contrary to the many scriptures. This would be interpretative suicide.

I have heard some use the scripture in John 6:39 and John 18:9 their reasoning to believe that every one that is truly in the LORD will never be lost and those believers who are lost were never truly one of the LORDs, to begin with. In understanding this text, we must first understand that the scriptures are in harmony, and they do not contradict one another. John 18:9 states, "That the saying might be fulfilled, which he spake, Of them which thou gavest me have I lost none (KJV);" and John 6:39 states, "And this is the Father's will which hath sent me, that of all which he hath given me I should lose nothing, but should raise it up again at the last day (KJV);" These two scriptures cannot stand alone, but John 6:39 must be understood by the next verse that states, "And this is the will of him that sent me, that everyone which seeth the Son, and believeth on him, may have everlasting life: and I will raise him up at the last day (John 6:40, KJV)." The key word is believed because to believe is attached to the obedience of the child of GOD. It is not that the LORD loses anyone, but it is the unbelief of the person that causes them to leave the LORD. It is the unbelief that causes a person to depart from the living GOD according to (Heb 3:12). Therefore, Jesus said why call ye me, Lord, Lord, and do not the things which I say (Luke 6:46, KJV)?

Even JESUS foretold of the events in the last days saying:

Then many will be led into sin, and they will betray one another and hate one another. And many false prophets will appear and deceive many, and because lawlessness will increase so much, the love of many will grow cold. But the person who endures to the end will be saved (Matthew 24:10-13, NET).

The first verse is speaking of a "falling away" from the faith. In the King James Version, it is translated as "shall many be offended" and in other translations, verse ten states, "many will fall away." The Greek word that is used for offended, fall away, and led into sin is "σκανδαλίζω" {skan-dal-id'-zo}, which means to put a stumbling block or impediment in the way, upon which another may trip and fall or to cause a person to begin to distrust and desert one whom he ought to trust and obey; to cause to fall away. This is congruent with Paul's teachings to them in Thessalonica when he stated, let no man deceive you by any means: for that day shall not come, except there comes a falling away first, and that man of sin be revealed, the son of perdition (2 Thessalonians 2:3, KJV). Furthermore, no child of the Most High GOD should take for granted the salvation provided by the LORD by delving into the erroneous doctrine of eternal security but rather, "Let us hold fast the profession of our faith without wavering because if we sin willfully after that we have received the knowledge of the truth, there remaineth no more sacrifice for sins (Hebrews 10:23,26, KJV)."

Furthermore, to elaborate on John 18:9, this scripture, along with John 6:39 has a technical meaning that can be understood by John 17:12 when it states, "When I was with them I kept them safe and watched over them in your name that you have given me. Not one of them was lost except the one destined for destruction, so that the scripture could be fulfilled (John 17:12, NET)." This scripture gives light to what is meant in John 16:39 and 18:9 that the LORD is talking about the apostles of the Lamb. He did not lose one of them except for Judas, who chose the path of destruction by betraying JESUS. Now the question must be asked if Judas was an apostle handpicked by JESUS and he betrayed him and lost his place then that is also the case for the believer that he can be lost after walking and believing in the LORD once before.

CHAPTER 4 UNDERSTANDING JOHN 20:17

Miseducation: *The Father is Jesus' God like every believer.*

John 20:17 "Jesus saith unto her, Touch me not; for I am not yet ascended to my Father: but go to my brethren, and say unto them, I ascend unto my Father, and your Father; and to my God, and your God. (KJV)"

The key to understanding John 20:17 is to read John in its entirety. As well as understand the whole plan of God. When Jesus states, "I ascend unto my Father…. and to my God" then we must know where Jesus came from. In John 1:1 it says, "In the beginning was the Word, and the Word was with God, and the **Word was God** (KJV)." Jesus was with God as his ultimate plan or hidden plan (musterion/mystery) and that is why 1 Timothy 3:16 states, "And without controversy great is the mystery (hidden plan) of godliness: God was manifest in the flesh, justified in the Spirit, seen of angels, preached unto the Gentiles, believed on in the world, received up into glory. Clearly, this is talking about Jesus which is the same one that was the Word of God. The Hebrew word "memra" means: "The **Word**," in the sense of the creative or directive **word** or speech of God manifesting His power in the world of matter or mind; a **term** used especially in the Targum as a substitute for "the Lord" when an anthropomorphic expression is to be avoided (Jewish Encyclopedia)."

This plan was that God would manifest himself into flesh to save mankind, and it was a plan before the world, i.e., Rev. 13:8 the Lamb slain from the foundation of the world; 1 Pet. 1:20 the Christ was foreordained before the foundation of the world; and 1 Cor. 2:7 we speak the wisdom of God in a mystery, even the hidden wisdom, which God ordained before the world unto our glory (KJV)." So now we know where he came from, which was the bosom of the Father according to (John 1:18) and so where else would he go back to?

    We still need more context, so in John 1:18 it says, "No man hath seen God at any time, the only begotten Son, which is in the bosom of the Father, he hath declared him (KJV)." First, we must notice that nobody has seen God because in John 4:24 "God is a Spirit (KJV)." Since God is a spirit, how could anyone see him? This is where Jesus comes to be seen as the manifestation of God, who was at one point the Word of God or a hidden plan of God that was not in a natural state but a spiritual thought process or plan that God had before the world was formed. When Jesus came, we must understand that the phrase "only begotten" is the Greek term "mono genos" and it means one of the same natures. Also, it is key to know that the scripture never said, "only begotten son." In the original Greek manuscripts, it says, **"only begotten God."** Since God is a spirit, then the only way God can come save man is to enter the natural realm as a man and who we know as the "only begotten God," and the one who was begotten came from the same nature or spirit as God but put God on display for us to see as Jesus the Christ. The word "declare" in John 1:18 means to put on display, or in other terms, Jesus was the face of God or the natural expression of the spirit of God. So, when Jesus "ascend unto his Father.... and to his God" he is going back into the spiritual essence of what God has always been.

We will go a little further. We also must understand the way Jesus speaks in scripture. Jesus states in John 16:25, "These things have I spoken unto you in proverbs: but the time cometh, when I shall no more speak unto you in proverbs, but I shall shew you plainly of the Father (KJV)." Jesus came not to make a reputation of himself. In Phil. 2:6,7 it states, "Who, being in the form of God, thought it not robbery to be equal with God: But made himself of no reputation, and took upon him the form of a servant, and was made in the likeness of men (KJV)." Jesus had to speak in subjugation to God because he did not come to be God, he came to be the Lamb slain for the sins of the world. But in John 20:17 he is speaking about returning to his original state but speaks in proverbs or what is considered cryptic language for the purpose of not making a reputation for himself as God even though he was in the form of God. God role on earth was not to be God but to be the Messiah. I work for a university as a recruiter; however, I am also a preacher. If I travel to another state to recruit for the university but confuse my roles, I will not successfully do what I came to do. God came to deal with sin as a son or a man and his roles were not confused. As Father he is creator, and he was not coming to create he was coming to destroy sin!

The explanation of John 20:17 is that it is at the end of the book of John the author is beginning to sum up the earthly ministry of the Messiah and now it is time for him to leave and go back to where he came from which was the bosom of the Father or back to what he was which was the Word of God that created the world according to John 1:1-3. Therefore, in 1 Cor. 15:24, Jesus is reconciling himself back to God. "Then cometh the end, when he shall have delivered up the kingdom to God, even the Father; when he shall have put down all rule and all authority and power." When that final enemy is defeated, there is no more need for a Lamb and the great reconciliation is when Jesus as man returns to spirit from the beginning because the flesh of Jesus was no more than a vehicle to carry the spirit of God as in Revelation 21:3 it calls him the tabernacle of God that dwelleth with man. Then the prophecy will be fulfilled in Zechariah 4:9, "And the LORD shall be king over all the earth: in that day shall there be one LORD, and his name one (KJV)." We know that in Rev 19:16, Jesus is called the King of Kings, but in Zec. 4:9 God is the King, but there is no confusion. There is one King in all the earth, and his name is Jesus, who is the Living God! John 20:17 must be understood not as a single scripture but interpreted through the entire book of John and the Bible. Therefore, if we go further down in the chapter in verse twenty-eight, "Thomas answered and said unto him, **My Lord and my God** (KJV)." This would be blasphemy if it were not true. Jesus does speak in proverbs but he does give hints to who he really is in the book of John at times in scriptures like: John 8:58 Before Abraham was, I am; 10:30 I and my Father are one; 12:45 he that seeth me seeth him that sent me; 14:7-9 he that hath seen me hath seen the Father; and most importantly 8:24 I said therefore unto you, that ye shall die in your sins: for if ye believe not that I am he, ye shall die in your sins (KJV)."

CHAPTER 5 ARE THERE APOSTLES TODAY?

Miseducation: *The LORD is still calling people to the office of the apostles today.*

This chapter is to clear up misunderstandings and prove the truth about whether there are apostles today or not. There has been much debate surrounding this subject, and there are many preachers today who proclaim they are apostles. So, to continue to seek true Biblical orthodoxy, we must search for the truth by allowing the scriptures to declare and prove what is rightly divided to strengthen Christians today. There is one thing that is clear about this subject, and that is there are only two kinds of apostles in the bible: true and false. 2 Corinthians 11:13 states, "For such are false apostles, deceitful workers, transforming themselves into the apostles of Christ (KJV)." It is clear that even in the infancy of the church there were many claiming to be apostles. This problem was even addressed in Revelation 2:2, when John recorded the words of our exalted Savior, "I know thy works, and thy labour, and thy patience, and how thou canst not bear them which are evil: and thou hast tried them which say they are apostles, and are not, and hast found them liars (KJV)." If this problem existed, then we should not be gullible to believe it is not happening now.

To analyze this subject appropriately, let us first start off with a definition of an apostle. Apostle means to be a delegate, messenger, or one who is sent forth with orders. It is specifically applied to the twelve apostles of Christ. The Greek word from which we get our English word apostles is "ἀπόστολος." This word can be translated in at least four ways in the scripture, which can be rendered: apostle, messenger, envoy, or one who is sent. I will show how the translation of this Greek word has confused many, and because it can be translated in more than one way then, it can be misleading to the novice reader of scripture. In modern times, people who love titles and want to appear as if they have some superior spiritual prowess above others will use this term loosely and justify it by pointing to the meaning of "one who is sent," which we will address later in the chapter. Let us look at the origin of the word from the Hebrew perspective as well to give a more adequate analysis of how the term is used. The term "apostle" from a Biblical Hebrew perspective is **"Shaliah or Shaliach."** The Hebrew description is that of a Jewish legal emissary or agent. The **"shaliaḥ"** performs an act of legal significance for the benefit of the sender, as opposed to him or herself. It means "one sent," but the authority and duration are much greater. A man's **"shaliah"** is like to himself, or it is as if the man is there himself speaking. The first shaliaḥ mentioned in the written scriptures is Eliezer, who was sent by Abraham to find a wife for Isaac. Hebrew principle of agency or Shaliach This particular concept, that of the shaliach (Strong's H7975 – one sent)[1] or fully-empowered agent of another person (what we would call a proxy in Common Law), was absolutely essential to the entire salvation plan of Jehovah for humanity. Without it, salvation would have been impossible and the entirety of creation pointless. The prototypical Biblical example of the duties and powers of a **shaliach** in Hebrew culture is found in the story of Eliezer, a servant of Abraham, who was sent to find a wife for Abraham's son, Isaac (Genesis 24). Eliezer had the same authority to bind his principals, Abraham, and Isaac, to the terms of a marriage covenant as if he were Abraham and Isaac themselves.

In a specialized sense when the patriarch as lord of his household deputized his trusted servant as his **malak** (his messenger or angel) the man was endowed with the authority and resources of his lord to represent him fully and transact business in his name. In Semitic thought this messenger-representative was conceived of as being personally — and in his very words — the presence of the sender."[2]

I will give examples of this towards the end of this article to clear up the confusion. But let us start with a more practical approach, I have compiled a list of qualifications that a person must pass to be considered an apostle. There are four qualifications by scripture that distinguish a person to be in the office of an apostle.

I. The Apostles were the foundation of the Church and formulated our doctrine:

Since the foundation is laid and the doctrine is already established, why would we need more apostles?

1. [KJV] **Ephesians 2:20** And are built upon the *foundation of the apostles* and prophets, Jesus Christ himself being the chief corner *stone*; (KJV)

2. ^{KJV} **John 17:20** Neither pray I for these alone, but for them also which shall *believe on me through their word*; (KJV)
3. ^{KJV} **Ephesians 3:4-5** [4] Whereby, when ye read, ye may understand my knowledge in the mystery of Christ) [5] Which in other ages was not made known unto the sons of men, as it is now *revealed unto his holy apostles* and prophets by the Spirit; (KJV)
4. ^{KJV} **Ephesians 4:11** And he gave some, apostles; and some, prophets; and some, evangelists; and some, pastors, and teachers; (KJV)

II. Apostles operated in all the gifts of the spirit performing signs and wonders:

Why do people who call themselves apostles today not operate as the twelve apostles in the Bible?

1. ^{KJV} **Acts 2:43** And fear came upon every soul: and *many wonders and signs were done by the apostles*. (KJV)
2. ^{KJV} **Acts 5:12** And by the hands of *the apostles were many signs and wonders* wrought among the people; (and they were all with one accord in Solomon's porch. (KJV)

III. Apostles were witnesses of the resurrection:

There is no one person today who calls themselves an apostle who has witnessed the resurrection of Jesus!

1. ^{KJV} **Acts 4:33** And with great power gave *the apostles witness of the resurrection* of the Lord Jesus: and great grace was upon them all. (KJV)
2. ^{KJV} **1 Corinthians 15:7-9** After that, he was seen of James; then of all the apostles. ⁸ And last of all he was seen of me also, as of one born out of due time. ⁹ For I am the least of the apostles, that am not meet to be called an apostle, because I persecuted the church of God. (KJV) This scripture supports and confirms Paul's apostleship.

IV. There are only twelve apostles:

We need to ask people who call themselves apostles today, "When did Jesus add you and subtract one of the original twelve apostles?"

1. ^{KJV} **Revelation 21:14** And the wall of the city had **twelve foundations,** and in them the names of the **twelve apostles of the Lamb.** (KJV)
2. **Acts 6:2** Then *the twelve* called the multitude of the disciples *unto them,* and said, It is not reason that we should leave the word of God and serve tables. (KJV)
3. ^{KJV} **1 Corinthians 15:5** And that he was seen of Cephas, then of the twelve: (KJV)
4. One of *the twelve:* Matt 26:14,47; Mk. 14:10,20,43; Lk. 22:47; Jn. 6:71; Jn. 20:24

V. The other kind of apostle mentioned in the Bible: (FALSE APOSTLES)

1. ^{KJV} **2 Corinthians 11:13** For such *are false apostles*, deceitful workers, transforming themselves into the apostles of Christ. (2Co 11:13 KJV)
2. ^{KJV} **Revelation 2:2** I know thy works, and thy labour, and thy patience, and how thou canst not bear them which are evil: and thou hast tried them which say they are apostles, and are not, and hast found them *liars:* (Rev 2:2 KJV)

To make sure we address all the issues concerning this subject, I must mention the other scriptures that come into question and is problematic to this subject. Some use Rom. 16:7 to say there are other apostles in the Bible besides the twelve, but this is misinterpreted by the rendering of the King James Version. In the KJV, Romans 16:7 states, "Salute Andronicus and Junia, my kinsmen, and my fellow prisoners, who are of note among the apostles, who also were in Christ before me (KJV)." This just means they were around them, not that they held the office of an apostle! The New English Translation gives a better translation, for it says, "Greet Andronicus and Junia, my compatriots, and my fellow prisoners. They are well known to the apostles, and they were in Christ before me (Romans 16:7, NET)."

In Acts 14:14, Barnabas is alluded to as an apostle and 1 Thes. 1:1 and 2:6 it seems as if Paul is declaring that Timothy and Silvanus are apostles. Here is where I will deal with translation and the difficulties when interpreting scripture. At the beginning of this article, I pointed out that the word apostle can mean one who is sent or messenger. Therefore, in Acts 14:14; 1 Thes. 1:1 and 2:6 it could read ones who are sent by Christ or messengers of Christ. For example, Philippians 2:25 reads, "Yet I supposed it necessary to send to you Epaphroditus, my brother, and companion in labour, and fellow soldier, but your **messenger**, and he that ministered to my wants (KJV)." The word messenger in this scripture is the same Greek word "ἀπόστολος," but in this particular scripture, it did not declare Epaphroditus, an apostle, and this is the same translation of "ἀπόστολος" that should have been given to describe Barnabas, Timothy, and Silvanus. Just to mention, the King James Version only uses the word messenger five times, and out of the five times, in Philippians 2:25 comes from "ἀπόστολος" and the other four times in Matt. 11:10; Mark 1:2; Luke 7:27 and 2 Cor. 12:7 it comes from the Greek word "ἄγγελος," which means, messenger, envoy, and one who is sent just like "ἀπόστολος" but nobody is calling themselves an angel as in a divine angel so why are people calling themselves apostles as in the office? Another example is John 13:16, "Verily, verily, I say unto you, the servant is not greater than his lord; neither he that is **sent** greater than he that sent him (KJV)." The word sent is also the Greek word "ἀπόστολος," but it uses a proper rendering. Therefore, people should not give themselves the title of an apostle today because headquarters only had twelve of those positions to be occupied and the jobs have been taken. If they want to call themselves an apostle according to the meaning of messenger or one who is sent then they are still incorrect because everyone who is saved is a messenger and sent of God because Romans 1:5 declares, "we have received grace and apostleship" but none of us are occupying the office of an apostle.

Regarding **Ephesians 4:11,** "And he gave some, apostles; and some, prophets; and some, evangelists; and some, pastors and teachers; (KJV)" we must understand this scripture through the lens of the building of the LORD's church. He did give some apostles; however, this was for the foundation of the building. He also gave some prophets which are also the foundation as Ephesians 2:20 states, "And are built upon the *foundation of the apostles* and prophets, Jesus Christ himself being the chief corner *stone;* (KJV). Paul said, "According to the grace of God, which is given unto me, as a wise masterbuilder, I have laid the foundation, and another buildeth thereon. But let every man take heed how he buildeth thereupon (1 Cor. 3:10, KJV)." Ministers today are only supposed to build upon the foundation because the apostles have already laid it. There are twenty-four seats in heaven for the 12 New Testament apostles and 12 Old Testament prophets. We must understand that if we use apostle in its simplest definition as one who is sent or messenger then everyone is an apostle according to Romans 1:5 because "we have received grace and apostleship." This will be the same as Joel 2:28 saying "your sons and daughters shall prophesy" but we are not all prophets. Furthermore, what the church calls the fivefold ministry is a term created by the English-speaking world. This term is made up and from a made-up term Christian ministers use it as if it is something they need or desire to operate in. This scripture is only a concise list of ministries the LORD has used to build His church. Extrabiblical terms have always tripped the Body of

Christ up because we try to fit in the terms. Now this term has become a doctrine but not of the Apostles of the Lamb or JESUS.

Furthermore, if the so called preachers today are apostles then why won't they do what the first apostles did in Acts chapter 4 verses 34 and 35: "Neither was there any among them that lacked: for as many as were possessors of lands or houses sold them, and brought the prices of the things that were sold, And laid them down at the apostles' feet: and distribution was made unto every man according as he had need (KJV)." The apostles of the Lamb were not capitalistic in their ministry but distributed all monies evenly to all believers that followed them so everyone can have the same socioeconomic status to eliminate any big I's and little U's. The apostles were also accountable to each other in that when there was a dispute among themselves about questionable behavior or doctrine they convene as they did in the book of Acts chapter 15. The self-proclaimed apostles today do not convene with other apostles to settle doctrinal matters because first all of there are no other apostles to consult with and they have no accountability and no one to challenge them as Paul challenged Peter in Galatians chapter 2 verse eleven.

In closing, we must understand that there are only twelve apostles of the Lamb and Paul is the choice apostle of Jesus that replaced Judas. The apostles knew the significance of having twelve apostles and that is why they tried to add one themselves by casting lots in Acts 1:26 and chose Matthias without consulting the Lord but Jesus chose Paul. If there was going to be more than twelve, then they would not have been concerned in filling Judas place. Therefore, if a person calls themselves an apostle in the sense of the office of an apostle, they are doing it in error or arrogance! If they do not meet the qualifications that are listed in roman numerals 1-4 then they must fit the description in number 5, FALSE APOSTLE! The Body of Christ cannot afford to allow this heretical doctrine to continue in the Church of the Living God. The early church tried them that called themselves apostles so why do the modern church allow this to continue? The taking on the title of an apostle has only come to fruition within the last decade, which proves it is a latter-day doctrine which is labeled as a doctrine of devils. Let us earnestly contend for the faith!

CHAPTER 6 WOMEN ROLE IN MINISTRY

__Miseducation:__ A women should not be allowed to preach from the pulpit. A woman should not be allowed to pastor. A woman should not be allowed to be a bishop. Women should be in silence.

---

1 Corinthians 14:34-35 Let your women keep silence in the church: for it is not permitted unto them to speak: but they are commanded to be under obedience, as also saith the law. And if they will learn anything let them ask their husbands at home: for it is a shame for women to speak in the church. (Rev 21:1 KJV)

What is the role of a woman in the church? Can they preach, teach or pastor a church? This was a question posed to me before. This is also a discussion that has been debated over for centuries. What is the role of a woman in the church? Women has often been discriminated against in the church among many denominations as well as other religion. The Bible has described women being used in many ways from the Old Testament through the New Testament. We see Deborah used as the first and only woman judge in the history of Israel, and this was not a mistake by man or in error; God divinely appointed her. In Judges 4:4 Deborah is not only described as a judge but as a prophetess and a judge. "And Deborah, a prophetess, the wife of Lapidoth, she judged Israel at that time" (KJV). We have in Romans 16:1 Phebe is working as a Deacon in the church at Cenchrea. Most ministries ascribe deacons to only men as if it is a gender-based term that can only describe a man to serve in that position. Romans 16:1 state, "I commend unto you Phebe our sister, which is a servant of the church which is at Cenchrea:" (KJV). The word servant in this scripture is "διάκονον" which can be translated as deacon or minister, where in other scriptures servant is the Greek word "δοῦλος." If a woman is a Deacon as Phebe was this does not mean she should be called deaconess because Deacon is not a gender specific term. In some Christian organizations women are called evangelist and men elders. This is genderizing Biblical terms that are ascribed to a gender but any servant of GOD regardless of their gender.

Deacon is not the only Biblical term that has been considered a masculine term but also the term Elder. In looking at the Biblical term "elder" it must be understood in its semantical range unless it be taken out of context. Elder comes from the Greek word πρεσβύτερος (presbuteros {pres-boo'-ter-os}) which means 1) elder, of age, or 1a) a term of rank or office.[1] When reading the Holy Scriptures, it must be determined which use is being expressed. Once the understanding of this word is determined then there can be an explanation to whether it can be used regarding women in church government. Looking at some key scriptures as in 1 Timothy we read:

> 1 Timothy 5:1, 2 Rebuke not an elder, but intreat him as a father; and the younger men as brethren; 2 The elder women as mothers; the younger as sisters, with all purity. (KJV)

In chapter 5, verses 1 and 2, Paul is instructing a young Pastor on how to be respectful to the older saints to be able to not only show respect but wisdom in the pastorate. This is the term "elder" being used regarding the age of a person. I remember having a conversation with a young pastor in his early thirties, and he was upset because an older woman gave him some instructions. He took offense to it because he was miseducated in this text and felt like the older lady had no right to rebuke him as an elder. But this text supports the lady as his elder and he was supposed to entreat her as a mother as Paul instructed Timothy. Later in chapter 5 of 1 Timothy, there is a change of usage of the term elder in verses 16-19.

> 1 Timothy 5:17-19 17 Let the elders that rule well be counted worthy of double honour, especially they who labour in the word and doctrine. 18 For the scripture saith, Thou shalt not muzzle the ox that treadeth out the corn. And, The labourer is worthy of his reward. 19 Against an elder receive not an accusation, but before two or three witnesses. (KJG)

Paul uses this opportunity to now instruct Timothy in dealing with leadership in the church and states that "elders" must be held with high esteem for their diligence in servitude and skillfulness in the Word of God. Elder here is understood as a term of rank or office.

After looking at the different uses of the Greek word "presbuteros" we now look at the word in how it is interchangeable with other words when looking at the word when dealing with the rank or office. Other scriptures that use elder regarding rank or office are as follows:

> Acts 20:17, 28 And from Miletus he sent to Ephesus, and called the elders of the church. 28 Take heed therefore unto yourselves, and to all the flock, over the which the Holy Ghost hath made you overseers, to feed the church of God, which he hath purchased with his own blood. (KJV)

> 1 Peter 5:1, 2 The elders which are among you I exhort, who am also an elder, and a witness of the sufferings of Christ, and also a partaker of the glory that shall be revealed: 2 Feed the flock of God which is among you, taking the oversight thereof, not by constraint, but willingly; not for filthy lucre, but of a ready mind; (KJG)

In these texts in Acts and 1 Peter, we notice that "elders, overseers and pastors" are interchangeable. Feed in Acts 20:28 and 1 Peter 5:2 is the Greek word ποιμαίνω poimaino {poy-mah'-ee-no} which means: to feed, to tend a flock, keep sheep 1a) to rule, govern or pastor.[2] The word pastor in the scriptures uses the same Greek word. Overseer is another word for Bishop. So, in other words, if a woman can be a pastor, then a woman can be an elder since these words are interchangeable. Since the Biblical meaning of the word pastor means to feed or, in other words, teach, then a woman who teaches can be called an elder. There are many pastors within the church although there is a senior pastor. A person is an Elder by knowledge, a pastor because they teach saints their knowledge and a person is an Overseer or Bishop when watching over the assembly of saints.

Furthermore, if women cannot be Elders in church government as a term of rank or office, then they should not be allowed to pray for people within the church to overcome sickness because in the book of James, it says that only the elders can pray for the sick.

> James 5:14 Is any sick among you? let him call for the elders of the church; and let them pray over him, anointing him with oil in the name of the Lord: (KJV)

Let us look at other women the LORD used greatly in the Bible: In Exodus 15:20, **Miriam is a prophetess**; in 2 Kings 22:14 **Huldah is a prophetess**; Nehemiah 6:14 **Noadiah is a prophetess**; in Luke 2:36, **Anna is a prophetess**, in Acts 21:8-10 Philip had **four daughters that prophesied. Lydia was an evangelist** in Acts 16 11-14, **Priscilla was an evangelist** in Acts 18:2-3; 18:18, 18:19, 18:26; Romans 16:3-4; 1Corinthians 16:19; 2 Timothy 4:19, and in Romans 16:7-12 Paul mentioned a list of women that were used by God in their labor work in the Lord.

Another reference to women in the scriptures that many overlook is in Acts 17:4 where it says, "And some of them believed, and consorted with Paul and Silas; and of the devout Greeks a great multitude, and of the chief women not a few (KJV). In this text the Jews that were in Thessalonica whom Paul ministered to believed and began to follow not only Paul and Silas but it mentioned "chief women" which according to the Koine Greek word "πρώτων" can be translated as chief or leading women and not only were they leading women but there were a large number of them because the scriptures states, "not few."

But let us look at the real problem with people not accepting women as teachers or pastors in the New Testament church. It usually comes from a misinterpretation of scriptures that has caused some churches and organizations to oppress women in ministry or men who suffer from gender insecurity and are chauvinistic. 1 Timothy 2:12 and 1 Timothy 3:1-2 are the main scriptures that are used to oppress women. 1 Timothy 2:12 in the King James Version states, "But I suffer not a woman to teach, nor to usurp authority over the man, but to be in silence." 1 Timothy 3:1-2 in the King James Version states, "This is a true saying, if a man desire the office of a bishop, he desireth a good work. A bishop then must be blameless, the husband of one wife, vigilant, sober, of good behaviour, given to hospitality, apt to teach."

Let us look at 1 Timothy 3:1-2 a little closer. The word that was translated as man in the KJV is the Greek word "τις," this word should not be translated as man. The translation of this Greek word is certain one, someone, or anyone. So, the correct rendering of 1 Tim. 3:1 should read, "This is a true saying, if a (certain one, anyone or someone) desire the office of an overseer." Also, in verse one, we have the present active indicative 3-person singular verb "ἐπιθυμεῖ" that can be translated (he, she, it desires), but the translators chose to use the pronoun he because Paul was talking to Timothy which is a man, and it was appropriate to use he. This does not teach that only a man can be an overseer or pastor, but anyone, someone, or a certain one can be an overseer. This was a letter to a man who was an overseer/pastor, and that is the explanation of verse two. It is irresponsible to take a letter written to a male pastor in the 1st or 2nd century and use it to formulate a doctrine to exclude women from pastoring a church.

Let us look at 1 Timothy 2:12 now. "But I suffer not a woman to teach, nor to usurp authority over the man, but to be in silence." The word translated as a woman is the Greek word "γυναικὶ," which is most of the time translated as a wife and the word translated as man is the Greek word "ἀνδρός" which is most of the time translated as husband as in 1 Tim. 3:2. In the text, 1 Tim. 2:11-15, is clearly speaking about the order of the relationship between a husband and a wife because it gives an example of Adam and Eve. Through the many scriptures that mention women being used as prophetesses, deacons, ministers, judges, and evangelists, women obviously taught and not to women only. So, in 1 Timothy 2:12, it is not hindering women from teaching but remaining humble and submitted to their husbands even if they are preachers of the gospel. This scripture should appropriately be rendered, "But I suffer not a wife to teach, nor usurp authority over the **husband**...."

We must understand that God said that he will use not only men but also women in this New Covenant church. Joel 2:28 states, "I will pour out my spirit upon all flesh, and your sons and your daughters shall prophesy...", Acts 2:17-18 states, "I will pour out of my Spirit upon all flesh: and your sons and your daughters shall prophesy, 18 And on my servants and on my handmaidens (women) I will pour out in those days of my Spirit; and they shall prophesy..." Notice that the text did not say that he would pour out his spirit on the male gender for them to prophesy but on man and woman. In case there is a misunderstanding of what the word prophesy means to speak forth by divine inspiration. These scriptures are clear unless a man is suffering from gender insecurity, chauvinism, or a bigot. We must conclude that it is supported by scripture, and that is "There is neither Jew nor Greek, there is neither bond nor free, there is neither male nor female: for ye are all one in Christ Jesus (Gal. 3:28, KJV)."

CHAPTER 7 A NEW HEAVEN AND A NEW EARTH

Miseducation: The saints of GOD will live in the new heaven and those who never knew of the LORD but were good people will live in the new earth.

> *Revelation 21:1 And I saw a new heaven and a new earth: for the first heaven and the first earth were passed away; and there was no more sea. (Rev 21:1 KJV)*

In this apocryphal text of John, he describes what he saw as a new heaven and a new earth. This text has been interpreted in diverse ways, and for this reason, I write to try to bring more clarity to the text. It is clear in this text, if read in its entirety that the new heaven and new earth that John referred to was previously there because they replaced the "first heaven and the earth." The confusion comes in when people read the word heaven. Heaven is the Greek word "**οὐρανός** ouranos" **and** is translated as heaven or sky. Its lexical definition is:

1) the vaulted expanse of the sky with all things visible in it 1a) the universe, the world 1b) the aerial heavens or sky, the region where the clouds and the tempests gather, and where thunder and lightning are produced 1c) the sidereal or starry heavens 2) the region above the sidereal heavens, the seat of order of things eternal and consummately perfect were God dwells and other heavenly beings.[1]

Heaven and Earth (Sky and Earth)

If we look at the way John uses the term heaven, he uses it literally as the sky because out of this new heaven or sky came a city called Jerusalem that descended, and John describes this city as a future place of habitation on the new earth for the saints of God in chapter 21 of Revelation. It does not describe heaven as a place of habitation but rather a sky where a city descended upon a new earth. The new sky replaced the old, damaged sky and the new earth replaced the old, damaged earth. Furthermore, Revelation 21:1 corresponds with *Isaiah 65:17 For, behold, I create new heavens and a new earth: and the former shall not be remembered, nor come into mind. (KJV)* In chapter 65, Isaiah describes a similar vision of John in Revelation chapter 21. It speaks of a new city and the inhabitants of it. Heaven and earth also are mentioned in the Genesis creation record, *"In the beginning God created the heaven and the earth." (Gen 1:1 KJV)*
In this related text the scripture is describing heaven and earth as the visible sky and the visible earth. Why would God have a need to create a new heaven in the sense of the spiritual or celestial realm when he is the one that inhabits it and where he abides is perfect. However, there is a need to create a new sky because with global warming, toxins, and everything that has damaged the air quality we would need a new sky to complement the new earth.

Where do the Saints live in eternity?

Chapter 5 of the Book of Matthew gives a plainer explanation of where the children of God will abide.

[3] Blessed are the **poor in spirit:** for theirs is the **kingdom of heaven.**

⁴ Blessed are they that mourn: for they shall be comforted.

⁵ Blessed are **the meek:** for they shall **inherit the earth**.

In looking at these texts, we should not confuse the "kingdom of heaven" and the "earth" as two different residences. The reason Matthew uses the term kingdom of heaven is because he was speaking to a Jewish audience that believed it was blasphemed to use the unutterable name of God. This is consistent throughout Matthew. The term Kingdom of heaven is the same as the Kingdom of God. For example, in Luke's version of the Beatitudes in chapter 6, verse twenty, he says, *"Blessed be ye poor: for yours is the kingdom of God"* because he is speaking to a Gentile audience. So, with this understanding, we cannot use the kingdom of heaven as an explanation of a residence for a different group of people in verse three from verse five. In verse five of Matthew chapter 5, we see a clear distinction of where the saints will live and that is on earth. The Beatitudes from verses 3 through 11 describe how a saint's characteristic is supposed to be blessed. The only people who have a right to inhabit the new eternal earth with the capital being Jerusalem are the children of God and it will not serve as some purgatory for those who were not bad enough to go to Hell or for those who did not know of Jesus but would have chosen him if they had a chance. Jesus is a just God and will not allow people to time to elapse on a person before the gospel is preached to every nation, creature, or creation (Matt 24:14; Mark 16:15; Col 1:23). The new earth with the new sky (heaven) would be the perfect habitation that we received a glimpse of in Genesis before the fall of Adam. We will have the same opportunity Adam and Eve had without the capability to sin.

Our glorified bodies will live on a new earth under the perfect government and eternal reign of God.

Heavenly Places

What about the scriptures that say we will be or are in heavenly places? When the scripture discusses saints in heavenly places as the book of Ephesians uses, they are not speaking of a residency but a state of being. A spiritual state of being that is contrary to what was experienced before a person was in Christ.

"Ephesians 2:6 And hath raised us up together, and made us sit together in heavenly places in Christ Jesus: (KJV)" "Ephesians 1:3 Blessed be the God and Father of our Lord Jesus Christ, who hath blessed us with all spiritual blessings in heavenly places in Christ: (Eph 1:3 KJV)"

In some versions, heavenly places are translated as heavenly realms because they are considered spiritual states and not physical places. God wants what he has in the spirit to be useful for us while we are in the natural. Ephesians 3:10 states, *"To the intent that now unto the principalities and powers in heavenly places might be known by the church the manifold wisdom of God, (Eph 3:10 KJV)"* It is useful to do the service of God if equipped with a spiritual understanding of what the job requires. So, the LORD gives us an opportunity to sit with him in those heavenly places. But we are there now, not later. Now, we are in heavenly places in a spiritual state of being, but in eternity, we will be in a new earthly place in a physical state of being.

Who Lives in Heaven?

We must understand that the Bible never declares a place of residency for the saints of God in heaven, but this is only something that has been passed down by tradition but has no Biblical validity. The Bible does declare that *"God is in heaven"* in Ecclesiastes 5:2 but we must understand this is a figurative understanding of where God lives because he does not have a physical address but in Biblical terminology, it explains a spiritual address as heaven or sky or above because he is higher than the heavens which are far above our natural senses. But God is a spirit that encompasses all the universe, and he is exalted above everything. When he works on earth, the Bible declares that he comes from above, but if we describe that in America, does that mean he comes from beneath in Australia? No, he comes from above there as well. He surrounds every part of any natural space. If the earth is God's footstool (Is. 66:1; Ac 7:49), then he must come from a higher place, as heaven or sky. When God spoke from heaven it was a voice from above or the sky (Dan 4:31; Mat 3:17; Mar 1:11; Jon 12:28; Rev 10:4; 11:12; 14:2,13; 18:4).

In conclusion, there is no evidence of the Bible declaring that heaven would be the saint's eternal place of residency. The Bible does declare that *"the meek shall inherit the earth."* (Matt. 5:5, KJV) Discussing where a saint goes after death is an entirely different subject, but the final place of residence is clear and not as the traditionalists believe, as we will go to a place called heaven. That has no Biblical foundation. Nobody dies and goes to heaven, but we will die and wake up and be walking in new Jerusalem on earth.

CHAPTER 8 UNDERSTANDING ISAIAH 53:1-5 & HEALING MINISTRY

Miseducation: *If you are a believer then you should not live with or die from any physical illness.*

> Isaiah 53 ¹Who hath believed our report? and to whom is the arm of the Lord revealed?
>
> ² For he shall grow up before him as a tender plant, and as a root out of a dry ground: he hath no form nor comeliness; and when we shall see him, there is no beauty that we should desire him.
>
> ³ He is despised and rejected of men; a man of sorrows and acquainted with grief: and we hid as it were our faces from him; he was despised, and we esteemed him not.
>
> ⁴ Surely he hath borne our griefs, and carried our sorrows: yet we did esteem him stricken, smitten of God, and afflicted.
>
> ⁵ But he was wounded for our transgressions, he was bruised for our iniquities: the chastisement of our peace was upon him; and with his stripes we are healed.

This scripture has been debated not for long but by the recent advancements of the heretical teachings of the faith movement or what is described as the charismatic movement. Those who would use these scriptures out of context only lead many to believe that the prophet Isaiah is teaching that believers have the right to physical healing by Christ because he came to heal our physical bodies. These erroneous teachers with a lack of knowledge of interpretation would make many believe that this scripture alludes to Jesus dying on the cross and caused physical healing to be a part of the package of the cross, and if they only have the faith to believe, they could be healed. This exegesis would show how this teaching cannot be true and give a more plausible explanation and interpretation of the ancient text.

Mistake of Interpretation: Jesus came to heal us from physical illnesses.

1. The faith teachers take verse four, which by the King James Version states, hath borne our griefs, and carried our sorrows," and has shown how griefs mean illnesses and sorrows mean pain, which is true. This truth, however, does not mean Jesus came to have physical healing as a gift of the cross, and every believer who has illnesses or physical pain should experience healing by faith. On the contrary, this scripture identifies what the messiah would do when he come to earth, and this is how, through the witness of scripture, we will know who the messiah is because he will be healing illnesses and pain through his ministry on earth. This is an identifier only. If we use a simple technique of hermeneutics or interpretation where, we will use scripture to

interpret scripture and realize that Matthew 8:16,17 teaches that Isaiah 53:4 is an identification scripture of how we are to know that Jesus was the Messiah.

¹⁶ When the even was come, they brought unto him many that were possessed with devils: and he cast out the spirits with his word, and healed all that were sick:

¹⁷ That it might be fulfilled which was spoken by Esaias the prophet, saying, Himself took our infirmities, and bare our sicknesses.

This interpretation is also strengthened by Isaiah's other identification scriptures of the messiah, which use physical healing as an identifier, such as Isaiah 61:1 and 2.

61 The Spirit of the Lord God is upon me; because the Lord hath anointed me to preach good tidings unto the meek; he hath sent me to bind up the brokenhearted, to proclaim liberty to the captives, and the opening of the prison to them that are bound;

² To proclaim the acceptable year of the Lord, and the day of vengeance of our God; to comfort all that mourn;

This is descriptive of what the messiah will do on earth. The Messiah came with the Spirit of the Lord God and was anointed or appointed to do as the listed ministries described in Isaiah 61:1 and 2. Jesus understood Isaiah was going to be the key book to prove his messianic claim because in Luke 48:17 and 18, he opened the book of Isaiah and read chapter 61 verses 1 and 2 and made the claim that Isaiah was speaking of him and proved it by doing what Isaiah said he will do by displaying physical healings, preaching, and many more signs and wonders. Clearly, the faith teachers do not read their Bible or understand it because if they did, they would not confuse the people of God by teaching physical healing is for every believer who has the faith to obtain it. They would understand that the prophetical teachings of Isaiah were to identify who the messiah is by what the messiah does.

2. The second mistake of the faith teachers is the misinterpretation of verse five. The faith teachers will use verse five as more proof that Jesus came to heal us of physical illnesses because of the statement, "and by his stripes we are healed." This is the careless mistake of not understanding that verse five is what is considered as a Hebrew parallel. A Hebrew parallel is a common literary feature of Hebrew poetry in the Old Testament is called parallelism, in which the words of two or more lines of text are related in some way. Transgressions and iniquities are parallel to each other and because we all sinned and came short of the glory of God (Rom. 3:23) then we did not have peace with God and by his stripes we were healed from that sin so we can have peace with God. Not healed from our physical sickness, illness, or pain because that is not what caused us to be in opposition with God, it was sin!

But he was wounded for our transgressions, he was bruised for our iniquities: the chastisement of our peace was upon him; and with his stripes we are healed.

Using simple hermeneutics again, all we need to do is find the scripture that uses physical healing to give us the interpretation of Isaiah 53:5. However, there is none, but we do have a scripture that gives us the interpretation that proves this scripture teaches about the healing of sin and that is 1 Peter 2:24.

24 Who his own self bare our sins in his own body on the tree, that we, being dead to sins, should live unto righteousness: by whose stripes ye were healed.

How could some who call themselves preachers and teachers make silly and careless mistakes in interpreting scriptures? The intent of the prophetical teachings of the Old Testament about the messiah was to give a wonderful description of how to identify the messiah. These scriptures were never intended to teach that after Jesus completed his earthly ministry, these wonderful works of physical healing, the raising of the dead, and many other miracles would continue as a common and consistent part of the Body of Christ. However, there are gifts of divine healing in the Body of Christ, but it is not for every believer to experience. If this is the case, who will be the dead in Christ that will be raised in 1 Thessalonians 4:16? Many Christians will die from physical failure of some sort but be raised incorruptible. The greatest healing a believer can receive is the healing of sin.

Healing does not come by how much faith the person in need of the healing possesses because in Jesus' early ministry, many were healed who did not have faith, and some who were healed were complimented because they had faith. Lazarus was a dead man who was raised from the dead. He could not have faith while he was dead but got raised anyway. This was just part of an identifier of what the Messiah would do while on earth. In John 9, the blind man that Jesus put mud in his eyes did not have faith that Jesus would heal him because he did not know that Jesus would approach him, but Jesus explained that he was blind and that the works of God be made manifest, and this was the purpose he came for (to do messianic ministry). I will not belabor the point because there is so much more that could be said on the subject and more errors to correct in the so-called faith movement. I wish we had a WORD movement instead of a so-called faith movement where preachers learned to be teachers and understand God's Word and erase the errors of their erroneous teachings leading people into the ditch!

Mistake of thinking that you are healed based upon how much faith you have.

We find in the Scriptures that Christ did not require faith for everyone, faith is not demanded as a precondition for one to receive a miracle. When faith was required, it was in Jesus, not necessarily that one believed they could be healed. The faith movement says faith is a condition for our healing. Those who are not healed failed because they did not have the required amount of faith for God to react. Healings were done in many ways. By the person's faith, by an intermediary praying for another, and by God himself with no required faith from the recipient.

Below are scriptures that show healings and miracles being done without the recipient having faith:

Matt. 8:5-10 It was the faith of the centurion that healed his own servant. If we apply this today those who have enough faith for their own healing can apply it to everyone else to be healed.

Mk.5:35-43 The daughter of Jairus was healed from their fathers faith

Mk.2:5 Jesus healed the paralytic not because of his faith but of the four men who carried him.

Lk.17:11-19 Jesus healed all of the 10 lepers as they were walking to go see the priest but only one returned to give thanks.

Jn.11 Jesus raised Lazarus from the dead certainly it was not Lazarus' faith he was dead, neither did anyone else believe it could occur then. It was done so they could believe. (Also, Lk8:54).

Lk.8:26-39 The demoniac of Gadarene was healed without asking before he could express his faith.

Lk.2:50-51 Jn.18:10 When peter cut of the ear of Malchus Jesus healed him without any faith present.

The Bible records Jesus doing more miracles without anyone exercising faith than with them having or demonstrating faith. He fed the 5,000 before he could teach them to give them an opportunity to believe. (Lk.9:13-14 Mt.14:17) even after they had seen his provision, they disbelieved again before the feeding of the 4,000 (Mt.15:33). When proclaimed faith teachers tell people their healing did not come because of their lack of faith, it is not consistent with Biblical teachings. If God depended on man for a certain level of faith to be healed or cured, then we all would be looking to ourselves for power instead of relying on God. This is man's philosophy and has nothing to do with Biblical faith.

Jesus performed miracles even with disbelief among the disciples. The disciples could heal a boy of epilepsy, unable to cast the demon out of a boy (Mt.17:14-21) he continues to do this and rebukes them for their unbelief, saying they need to pray and fast to see God move. In other words, you cannot just depend on the authority given to you, we need to depend on God.

In Mt.13:58, we are told, "he did not do many miracles there because of their lack of faith. However, he did lay hands on a few sick people and healed them Mk.6:5."

Of the thirty-five miracles recorded in the Gospel accounts, the faith of the recipient is exercised in only ten of the accounts. Healing of the lame man (Jn.5:1-9) the cleansing of a leper (Mt.8:2-4) healing of a man withered hand (Mt.9:2-8) the healing of the man born blind (Jn.9:1-7) healing the blindness of Bartimaeus (Mt.20:29-34) The women who had a blood flow (Mt.9:20-22; Mk.5:24-34) Peter who walked on water to Jesus (Mt.14:24-33) the miraculous catching of the fish (Lk.5:1-11) and the second miraculous catch (Jn.21:1-11) The cleansing of the 10 lepers of which only one had faith which was most likely developed due to the healing (Lk.17:11-19).

Jesus did not heal everyone always as Jn.5:1-15 v.3 is an example where the multitudes were gathered at the pool of Bethsaida with many suffering from illnesses, but Jesus picked only one to be healed. A blind and lame man JESUS chose, and the scripture did not mention any other. In verse three, the blind man acted on Christ's invitation, having no faith. He did not know it was Jesus who healed him until later in verses twelve and thirteen. How many times did Jesus go past the gate of the temple and not heal anyone? Why doesn't he heal everyone all the time? Why did he choose some who had faith and picked others who had no faith? Those involved in faith healing will have no answer for this, at least one that would be biblical.

CHAPTER 9 THE MISEDUCATION OF ROMANS 10:9 & THE SINNER'S PRAYER

Miseducation: The Roman Road of Salvation. People can be saved just by saying the sinner's prayer and repeating Romans 10:9.

> *That if thou shalt confess with thy mouth the Lord Jesus, and shalt believe in thine heart that God hath raised him from the dead, thou shalt be saved. (Rom 10:9 KJV)*

The error of many preachers and churches in this present time is that they use Romans 10:9 as a mode of salvation for many new believers. Romans 10:9 has been incorporated into what is known as the "Sinners Prayer." After saying the prayer, inclusive of Romans 10:9 the individual is proclaimed to be a born-again Christian. This lesson is an attempt to bring clarity to Romans 10:9 and its erroneous use and how many ministers have taken their liberty and, in their eisegesis of this text, they have robbed many new believers of the beautiful experience of the new birth. This lesson is to right the wrong of the miseducation of the abuse of Romans 10:9.

Law of First Mention

To begin, we must first look at what is known as the law of first mention. The law of first mention is a hermeneutical principle where the first-mentioned truth of a subject in the Bible sets the standard for understanding and will not change later. This law must be taken into consideration when looking at the mode of Romans 10:9, as some preachers will use it. Romans 10:9 does not follow the same principle as the mode of salvation first mentioned in the book of Acts when the church began. The Book of Acts is imperative to understanding the mode of salvation because it is the Genesis of the New Testament. The Book of Acts is the history book of the New Testament in how the church was birthed and how the apostles established the church of the Living God throughout the world. The Book of Acts describes the inception of the Body of Christ and, most importantly, how to become a part of Christ's church. In Acts chapter two we read about a convicting message delivered by the apostles who was led by Peter and when he had climaxed at a certain part of his message and stated, "Therefore let all the house of Israel know assuredly, that God hath made that same Jesus, whom ye have crucified, both Lord and Christ (Act 2:36 KJV)." The response from all that heard "said unto Peter and to the rest of the apostles, Men, and brethren, what shall we do (Act 2:37 KJV)?" Then, in Acts 2:38 was given the first recorded advice by the apostles on how to be born again. The instructions were, "Repent and be baptized every one of you in the name of Jesus Christ for the remission of sins, and ye shall receive the gift of the Holy Ghost (KJV)." The reason why this is significant is that not only Romans 10:9 is not consistent with the mode of salvation explained in Acts 2:38 but everywhere else in the Book of Acts where the apostles encountered people they used the same mode in Acts 2:38. In Acts 8:14-18 the apostles ministered to the Samaritans and it was explained that they had been baptized in the name of the Lord Jesus and was only in need of the Holy Spirit and after the laying on of hands they received the Holy Spirit. In Acts 10:44-48 the apostles ministered to the Gentiles in the house of Cornelius and as Peter spoke the word of God all that heard received the Holy Spirit and the circumcision was astonished, and they agreed that even though they received the gift of the Holy Spirit it was still imperative that they be baptized in the name of the LORD JESUS. Even Acts 8:27-39 shows how Philip ministered to the Ethiopian eunuch and preached Jesus to him and baptized him in water. Furthermore, the Book of Romans was an epistle (letter) to the church in Rome that was already established when the epistle was written, so we must assume that they were already introduced to the mode of salvation that was recorded in the Book of Acts. Why would Paul introduce a new doctrine of salvation that was not used in the inception of the church? We must take notice that the author of the book of Acts was Luke who accompanied Paul on most of his missionary journeys and since Paul was an integral part of the birth of the church and taught the mode of salvation to Apollos and his followers that it was imperative to be baptized in the name of the LORD Jesus and receive the Holy Spirit. This same Apollos was described as eloquent, mighty in the scriptures, instructed in the way of the Lord, and fervent in the spirit (Acts 18:24,25). Apollos taught diligently the things of the Lord and spoke boldly in the synagogue and convinced Jews by the scriptures that Jesus was the Messiah (Act 18:25-28). Since Apollos was already a believer and obviously was very influential then why would Paul question how was he baptized and if he received the Holy Spirit? More importantly, why did he command them to be baptized in the name of the LORD instead of telling them to confess with their mouth the Lord Jesus, and believe in thine heart that God hath raised him from the dead and thou shalt be saved according to Romans 10:9? The answer is that Romans 10:9 was not and is not a mode of salvation for the church of Christ. The law first mentioned shows a very strong case in the book of Acts in how salvation was instructed to the Samaritans, the Ethiopian eunuch, the Gentiles, and even those who already believe, like Apollos, that salvation took more than just confessing with your mouth and believing or even saying a sinner's prayer.

Romans 10: The Plea for Israel

> Brethren, **my heart's desire and prayer to God for Israel** is, that they might be saved. 2 For I bear them record that they have a zeal of God, but not according to knowledge. 3 For they being ignorant of God's righteousness, and going about to establish their own righteousness, have not submitted themselves unto the righteousness of God. 8 But what saith it? The word is nigh thee, even in thy mouth, and in thy heart: that is, the word of faith, which we preach; 9 That if thou shalt confess with thy mouth the Lord Jesus, and shalt believe in thine heart that God hath raised him from the dead, thou shalt be saved. (Rom 10:1-3,8,9 KJV)

In the narrative of Paul, he made it clear of his intentions. In verse one, he says, "Brethren, my heart's desire and prayed to God for Israel is that they might be saved (Rom 10:1 KJV)." Paul makes it clear that his declaration in chapter ten is concerning the nation of Israel. Paul was concerned for his fellow countrymen because his mission given to him by the LORD was to be an apostle and teacher to the Gentiles according to Romans 11:13; Galatians 2:8; 1 Timothy 2:7; and 2 Timothy 1:11. Although his ministry was to the Gentiles, he still had a great concern for the nation of Israel who was blind concerning the Messiah. Namely, two groups of Israel were the Pharisees and the Sadducees or, in other words, Hellenists or anti-Hellenists. The Pharisees did not believe that Jesus was LORD and the promised Messiah. The Sadducees did not believe in the resurrection of the dead because Deuteronomy 21:23 states, for he that is hanged is accursed of God and reiterated in Galatian 3:13 saying, "for it is written, cursed is everyone that hangeth on a tree: (Gal 3:13 KJV)." Romans 10:9 is a plea to Paul's fellow countrymen that if the Pharisees could confess with their mouths that Jesus was the Messiah that fulfilled Old Testament prophesies and that the Sadducees could believe that Jesus was raised from the dead then they would have the opportunity to take part of the great salvation that the LORD produced through his precarious death, burial, and resurrection. Paul describes Israel in the next chapter of Romans 11:25 as "blindness in part has happened to Israel" and this blindness was that Israel as a nation could not see who Jesus really was and therefore, his plea in Romans 10 is that if they could only confess and believe then this would lead them to the blessing of knowing how to obtain salvation.

Confession unto Salvations

Looking at the doctrine of Romans 10:9 a little further, many would say that the following verse, Romans 10:10, is further proof that Paul was teaching that confession is all a person needs to obtain salvation. "For with the heart man believeth unto righteousness; and with the mouth confession is made unto salvation (Rom 10:10 KJV)." If this was true, once again, it would have to line up with the rest of the scriptures, especially the book of Acts. In Acts 2:21 it says, "And it shall come to pass, that whosoever shall call on the name of the Lord shall be saved (Act 2:21 KJV)." However, we must notice that the statement in Acts 2:21 is followed by many other words to the extent that the crowd that heard did believe and asked what they do, and the question was answered by the apostles with the command to be baptized in the name of Jesus for the remission of sins. So, we must look at the terms "thou shalt be saved;" "unto salvation;" and "shall be saved (Rom. 10:9,10; Acts 2:21)." The problem with using these texts to proclaim that an individual is saved is that the verb tense in Romans 10:9 and Acts 2:21 is both in the future tense. The Future Tense is like the English future tense, the Greek future talks about an anticipated action or a certain happening that will occur at some time in the future. So, Romans 10:9 states, "thou shalt be saved" which means that the confession does not give salvation but rather leads to it just like Acts 2:21 where the verb is also in the future tense so when it was stated, "that whosoever shall call on the name of the Lord shall be saved" this was evident that it was not immediate because if it was immediate salvation then the people that believed would not have asked "what shall we do?" The other statement in Romans 10:10, "unto salvation" is in the present tense, and the present tense usually denotes a continuous kind of action and shows 'action in progress' or a state of persistence. The Greek verb for salvation is σωτηρίαν which is the verb that follows the verb believeth (πιστεύεται) which is also in the present tense and is understood as an action of continuous believeth which is to be understood as faith that produces faithfulness, trust that produce trustworthiness, fidelity, and commitment and this leads to obeying the commandments of the LORD and the apostles to be baptized in the name of the LORD and receive the Holy Spirit. The problem with "unto salvation" is it doesn't put you into anything unless your belief produces obedience and completes the process described in Acts 2:38. I hope that this lesson has brought some clarity in how Romans 10:9 is supposed to be interpreted and how the use of this text as a mode of salvation is a product of miseducation.

Rapid Mass Salvation

This unbiblical formula for salvation was no more than a man-made solution to sold-out crowds of crusade preachers that preached to stadiums full of people and instead of them performing an exhausting number of baptisms and or directing them to local churches of the cities they passed through this became convenient to them just to have the masses repeat after the preacher and afterward have a celebration of mass manipulation. The historical development of the Sinner's Prayer can be traced to the late nineteenth and early twentieth centuries. As evangelists began to speak to extremely large crowds, they trained personal workers to aid with the crowds of people responding to invitations to the altar or what many call altar calls. They felt that they needed to develop a systemized presentation of the gospel and to aid the many people who felt compelled to answer the call to the altar for salvation, so the system of the sinner's prayer arose. Over time, a prayer of commitment became a part of this presentation of systematic theology. A theologian and author by the name of J.I. Packer describes the sinner's prayer as "the American production line mentality applied to evangelism."[1] The sinner's prayer represented a quick and effortless way to deal with individual seekers during a large meeting to not bottle-neck the services and put salvation on microwave speed. It is, however, a novel approach in evangelism. My research shows that the Sinner's Prayer was not popularized until late into the twentieth century, possibly as late as the 1940s or even the early 1950s. The Sinner's Prayer has many forms and variations but is usually worded in a similar fashion to the following example taken from Billy Graham's evangelistic tract, "Steps to Peace with God." "Dear Lord Jesus, I know that I am sinful, and I need Your forgiveness. I believe that you died to pay the penalty for my sin. I want to turn from my sinful nature and follow You instead. I invite You to come into my heart and life. In Jesus' Name. Amen."[2]

    In his evaluation of the Sinner's Prayer in connection with the public invitation, Elliff writes, "The 'sinner's prayer,' as we have come to see it, has three elements: (1) a mere acknowledgment of sin, which is not the same as repentance, (2) a belief in the act of Christ's death, which is far removed from trust in his person and work. and (3) an 'inviting Christ into the life.' The last phrase hangs on nothing biblical (though John 1:12 and Rev. 3:20 are used, out of context, for its basis)."[3] Elliff is further frustrated how altar call respondents who have prayed the Sinner's Prayer are then introduced as being "in Christ." He believes that to ensure persons of their salvation based upon this criterion is a grave error, going as far as to say, "So we seal people in deception..."[3]

The dangers as registered by Ehrhard are (1) The danger of promoting something that is not promoted in Scripture, (2) The danger of eliciting an emotional response based upon the personality of the speaker or the persuasion of the appeal, (3) The danger of confusing the "coming forward" with salvation., (4) The danger of counting great numbers who only discredit their profession by their lives, (5) The danger of giving assurance to those who are unconverted.[4]

CHAPTER 10 THE NECESSITY OF WATER BAPTISM

Miseducation: Water baptism is not necessary for salvation. It is just an outward declaration of an inward faith.

Can any man forbid water, that these should not be baptized, which have received the Holy Ghost as well as we? (Acts 10:47 KJV)

This writing is to address the many contemporary theologians with modern interpretations based on their philosophy. This is my many efforts in pleading with my fellow brothers and sisters to embrace Christianity in its purest form from the early conception of the Church and not give heed to many ideologies that have crept into the church of the Living God. In **Colossians 2:8** Paul states, "Beware lest any man spoil you through philosophy and vain deceit, after the tradition of men, after the rudiments of the world, and not after Christ." (Col 2:8 KJV) We are living in a time when people want to explain what Jesus said instead of obeying what he said. The subject of whether water baptism is necessary for salvation was foreign to a first-century church. For obedience is a requirement above all things and "to obey is better than sacrifice (1 Sam. 15:22)." We need to learn to "bring every thought into the obedience of Christ…. (2 Cor. 10:5,6) and "lean not to our own understanding…. (Prov. 3:5,6)." It is mind-blowing that some would question the validity of the necessity of baptism. Early Christians never had the thought process that baptism was rudimentary. No one ever raised the question then and it would have been strange to do so. Only this rebellious generation that lacks scriptural and spiritual integrity is where these inquiries come from. Questioning baptism would be like questioning whether it is necessary to pray, whether corporate worship is necessary, whether preaching is necessary, and whether the Bible is necessary. "Baptism occupied a place of great importance in the Christian community of the first century and was regarded as essential to the new birth and to membership in the Kingdom of God."[1]

Is water baptism necessary?

The answer is a resounding YES! **Mark 16:16 Whoever believes and is <u>baptized</u> will be saved; whoever does not believe will be condemned (NAB).** This was the New Testament pattern (see also Acts 2:41; 8:12, 35-37). Baptism marked a complete break with the past and a full entrance into Christ and His church. Baptism was simultaneously an act of faith as well as an expression of faith. Baptism is not a work or deed it is a commandment. As I mentioned in the introduction, obedience is a requirement to salvation, and if Jesus says do it, then that makes it a necessity. **John 14:15** If ye love me, keep my commandments. **Luke 6:46** And why call ye me, Lord, Lord, and do not the things which I say? I know some will say that they are not teaching to be baptized, and people should be. This does not make sense because if a person is teaching that it is not a requirement then there is no need. But it is a fact that holiness, loving people, and peaceful actions are not taught as necessities to salvation but **Hebrews 12:14** states, "Follow peace with all *men*, and holiness, without which no man shall see the Lord:" I do not understand how people get around the idea that baptism is not required when Jesus made it plain and clear. Baptism is for the remission of sins according to Acts 2:38. The book of Acts is the history of the beginning of the church and when the Apostles began preaching on the Day of Pentecost the people in the crowd stated in **Acts 2:37** "Now when they heard *this*, they were pricked in their heart, and said unto Peter and to the rest of the apostles, Men, *and* brethren, what shall we do?" Obviously, the people had believed in the preaching of the Apostles but wanted instructions on what to do and this is where the Apostles introduced the plan of salvation to the world. **Acts 2:38** Then Peter said unto them, Repent, and be baptized every one of you in the name of Jesus Christ for the remission of sins, and ye shall receive the gift of the Holy Ghost. Many say this scripture should appropriately be rendered, repent, and be baptized because your sins have been remitted. This confusion of interpretation is based on the preposition "εἰς." The phrase "εἰς ἄφεσιν τῶν ἁμαρτιῶν" in Acts 2:38 can only be rendered "for the remission of sins" according to Dana and Manley in his book, A Manual Grammar of the Greek New Testament.

"When one considers in Acts 2:38 repentance as self-renunciation and baptism as a public expression of self-surrender and self-dedication to Christ, which significance it certainly had in the first century, the expression εἰς ἄφεσιν τῶν ἁμαρτιῶν may mean for the purpose of the remission of sins."[2]

"It is possible that to a first-century Jewish audience (as well as to Peter), the idea of baptism might incorporate both the spiritual reality and the physical symbol. That Peter connects both closely in his thinking is clear from other passages such as Acts 10:47 and 11:15-16. If this interpretation is correct, then Acts 2:38 is saying little about the specific theological relationship between the symbol and the reality, only that historically they were viewed together."[3]

Baptism of the First Century

The image below is a page from the original Encyclopedia Britannica that was published in 1768. I want to share the entry on baptism because, after this edition, the entry was not published the same, but this original gives light to the first-century church mode of baptism and the theology behind the reason baptism was so important to them before so many after the apostles changed the view of baptism and meaning.

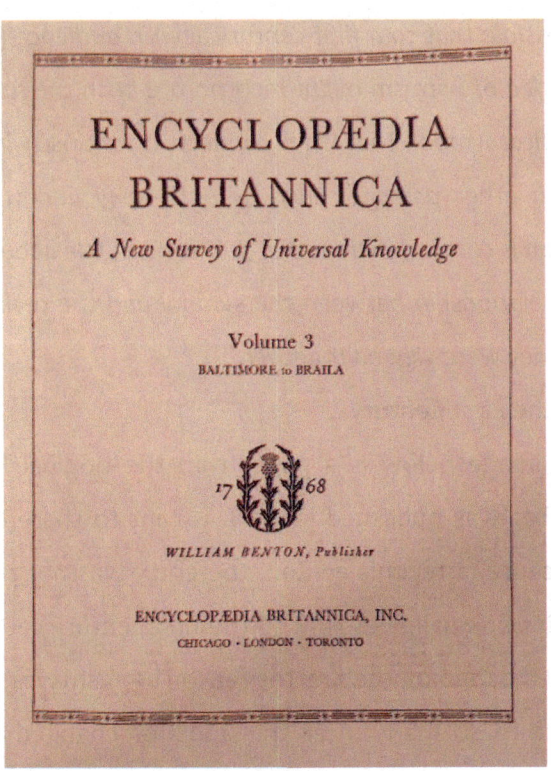

On page 82 of the 1768 Encyclopedia Britannica, under the subtitle **Jewish and Christian Baptism,** it states:

"The act itself took place without special preparation, as soon as the new convert confessed his faith in Christ and desired to become a member of the community: the baptism of the eunuch of Queen Candace (Acts.viii.38) is a good instance of this. Everywhere in the oldest sources it is said that baptism takes place "in the name of Jesus."[4]

Then, under the subtitle **The Apostolic Age,** it speaks to the necessity of water baptism as viewed by the first-century church. It says:

"Whether the Judaic primitive community formulated special theological ideas about baptism, we are not informed, and no probable conjecture enables us to infer that it was so. On the other hand, with the Apostle Paul, we come upon a developed sacramental theology. In I Cor. X., baptism appears as a sacrament already foreshadowed in the Old Testament and Rom. Vi. A fully articulated doctrine of the nature of baptism is produced in connection with the question of the Christian relation to sin. When in the ceremony, the candidate for baptism is submerged under water, he is thereby buried with Christ and dies with him, i.e., this submersion in water is for the Apostle, not merely a symbol of purification, nor only a symbol of being buried, but a real act of wonderful effect. The candidate for baptism experiences actually and genuinely the death of Jesus in his own body and is likewise actually laid in the grave, as Jesus lay in the grave. And thereby, the saving effect of these events, too, is transferred to him. He dies and, in doing so, pays to sin the tribute due: for the wages of sin is death. When he appears again from the water, the resurrection of Christ becomes his. He, who was dead, awakens to a new life but under conditions quite different from those that governed his mode of life hitherto. If till then the world-encircling power of sin exercised its dominion in the flesh without restraint, now that is possible no more. The flesh, dead in the sacramental union with Christ, has become free from the power of sin, which till now worked upon it with the force of a law of nature. As Christ rose from the dead through the spirit of God, which gave him life, so too is the baptized Christian equipped with the new life principle of the divine spirit and can fulfill the ordinance of the law (Romans 8:4). He is a new creature: the old man is dead, and all has become new (2 Corinthians 5:17). How realistically the effect of baptism is conceived is clear also from a curious custom which was the practice in Corinth (I Corinthians 15:29).["][5]

In the Hebrew version of the Gospel of Matthew, chapter 28, verse 19 is translated only as "Go," and then in verse 20, it says, "and teach them to carry out all things which I have commanded you forever."[6]

I have listed several arguments that have come into the Body of Christ about baptism way after the second century.

Arguments about Baptism

Argument 1: People argue the validity of water baptism as a necessity of salvation based on many believers. One of the most ridiculous reasons is the "deathbed confession." Mind you, "death bed confession" is not a doctrine taught by any apostle of the Lamb, nor is it Biblical. People take this from the event of their on the cross Luke 23:42,43. This was before the Body of Christ even existed and was not a New Testament doctrine on an alternative way of salvation. If that were the case, everybody would live however they wanted to, and then when it was time to expire, they would repent. Let us face it: everybody who feels their life is escaping them has a heightened sense of reality and sensitivity to their mortality and wants to repent. Repentance is a gift (Acts 11:18). But God can save anyone he wants to save when he wants to save them despite their acts, but that is called Divine Providence. Jesus forgave plenty of people of their sins many times while he was walking on Earth. There will be plenty of people who will be saved based on the mercy of God, but that does not mean we teach anything contrary to what he has established for the New Testament church and omit the necessity of water baptism.

Argument 2: Some argue that in John 3:5, Jesus did not mean water when he said, "except a man be born of the water..." This is certainly foolish because the Greek word **"ὕδωρ"** means water, and if it doesn't mean water in John 3:5, then it doesn't mean water in Acts 8:36 when it states, "See, *here is* water; what doth hinder me to be baptized" and it doesn't mean water in Jn. 2:7-9 when Jesus turned water into wine.

Argument 3: Some argue that baptism is an outward declaration of an inward faith just to show others that you have become a Christian. This is also another fallacy that has no Biblical validity because in Acts 8 in the story of the Ethiopian eunuch, who was the Ethiopian declaring his faith to when he asked Phillip the question, "See, here is water; what doth hinder me to be baptized (Acts 8:36)?" If baptism was not essential to salvation, then what was his purpose of asking about being baptized?

Argument 4: Baptism is just a work, and we cannot be saved by works. **Ephesians 2:8,9** "For by grace are ye saved through faith; and that not of yourselves: *it is* the gift of God: Not of works, lest any man should boast." Also, we are "justified by faith (Rom. 5:1). These scriptures are true, but the problem is the eisegesis people do in interpreting them and not considering the other scriptures. First, baptism is not considered a work in the scripture. Works are clearly described in the book of James 2:14-26. Primarily works are described as deeds or good deeds toward others in James 2:15. But for the sake of conversation, then we will look at baptism as a work, and if so, then we will read, "[17] So also faith of itself, if it does not have works, is dead. [20] Do you want proof, you ignoramus, that faith without works is useless? [24] You see that a man is justified by works, and not by faith alone (NABRE)." What more can be said for those who feel we are only saved by grace or faith? Please do not be an ignoramus. Being saved by grace is not saying by faith you are saved but grace. Grace means to have an undeserved divine endowment. We are saved by grace because we deserve to go to hell and pay for our sins, but Jesus took away sin by dying on the cross for the penalty of sin. We do not deserve that, but he has made salvation possible by this and when we come into covenant with him, we receive something undeserved. That is grace, and we are saved by it, but Eph. 2:8 does not inform us how we come into covenant or receive this undeserved gift. What more can be said for those who feel we are only saved by grace or faith? Please do not be an ignoramus.

Argument 5: This last argument that I have come to know is that in **John 3:5**, Jesus was talking about water as in the amniotic fluid that is in a woman during pregnancy and when the baby is ready to come out, what is commonly known as "water breaks." This, to me, is amusing, to say the least, because anyone who is educated knows that the fluid is not even water, although it has a water base. *Premature rupture of membranes* is what the fluid is that comes out, but even if it is water, Jesus was not alluding to a natural birth as Nicodemus was.

Also, if Jesus was not talking about a physical baptism in water, he was not talking about a spiritual one either. He mentioned that a person is born of the water and spirit. If it were spirit birth that was only needed, then he would not have included being born of the water. A person who uses this argument is reaching for anything to explain away the authenticity of water baptism. Murray states, "If Jn. 3:5 does not express the necessity of water in the sense of necessitas medii, then it also does not stress the necessity of the means, or better the Mediator, who is the Spirit."[7]

Argument 6: Many say that baptism is only a ceremony just like circumcision is in the Old Testament and is only typology. This is true in a sense. But let me point out that Genesis 17:14 says, "And the uncircumcised man child whose flesh of his foreskin is not circumcised, that soul shall be cut off from his people; he hath broken my covenant." So even though circumcision had no power to save Israel, God still said he would cut off the men who were not circumcised. This is the same with water baptism; if God ordained it and is a ceremonial covenant, then it is a requirement as well because, as it was stated in Gen. 17:14, the person who didn't get circumcised will be cut off then Jesus said in Mark **16:16** that " **Mark 16:16** Whoever believes and is baptized will be saved; whoever does not believe will be condemned (NAB)." The Bible does allude to baptism to be typology as well in Rom. 6:3-5 and Col. 2:11-12 but only to compare the physical action to the impact of our spiritual nature.

Argument 7: Paul did not baptize is another argument due to 1 Corinthians 1:14 when it says, "I thank God that I baptized none of you, but Crispus and Gaius." However, he did question the mode of baptism of Apollos in Acts 19:3-6 when saying, "And he said unto them, unto what then were ye baptized? And they said, Unto John's baptism. Then said Paul, John verily baptized with the baptism of repentance, saying unto the people, that they should believe on him which should come after him, that is, on Christ Jesus. When they heard this, they were baptized in the name of the Lord Jesus. And when Paul had laid his hands upon them, the Holy Ghost came on them; and they spake with tongues and prophesied."

CHAPTER 11 HOLY SPIRIT BAPTISM

Miseducation: *The holy spirit is automatically given to every believer in their profession of faith.*

I indeed have baptized you with water: but he shall baptize you with the Holy Ghost. (Mark 1:8 KJV)

But the Comforter, which is the Holy Ghost, whom the Father will send in my name, he shall teach you all things, and bring all things to your remembrance, whatsoever I have said unto you. (John 14:26 KJV)

But ye shall receive power, after that the Holy Ghost is come upon you: and ye shall be witnesses unto me both in Jerusalem, and in all Judaea, and in Samaria, and unto the uttermost part of the earth. (Acts 1:8 KJV)

The text found in Mark 1:8 discusses an experience that will come to the believer in the form of a baptism, which means to be fully immersed. It is the immersion of GOD's spirit, which is holy, to help the believer in fulfilling Acts 1:8 to empower the believer. The foretelling of this baptism was to prepare the disciples of Christ for the great phenomenon that would take place on the Day of Pentecost. They understood it as something that would guide them, teach, and bring an understanding of GOD's will, as well as empower them to do GOD's will. They only did not know how it would come as they were instructed to "not depart from Jerusalem, but wait for the promise of the Father, which, saith he, ye have heard of me. For John truly baptized with water, but ye shall be baptized with the Holy Ghost, not many days hence (Acts 1:4-5 KJV)."

The understanding of the baptism of the Holy Spirit is much debated. There are many theories, such as that it is automatically given to the believer, that tongues were only for the first-century church, and that tongues are a gift of the Holy Spirit and not for everyone to experience. It is important to mention that this chapter does not equate tongues with the Holy Spirit because the Holy Spirit is much more than speaking in tongues. I heard Johnny James (The Walking Bible) state, "If you buy a pair of shoes, the tongues come with it, and if you buy shoes that do not have tongues, it is considered a loafer. Tongues are not the Holy Spirit, but if you receive the Holy Spirit, the tongues come with it, and if it does not, it is a loafer." This chapter discusses what happens when a believer receives the Holy Spirit and not all that the Holy Spirit does once a believer has it.

In the discussion of the Holy Spirit, we will explore how the early church describes the baptism of the Holy Spirit or, in other words, what the scripture says about what happens when a believer receives the Holy Spirit. Many would argue that the Holy Spirit is given to believers when they become born again or receive the Lord as their savior. This is quite challenging to believe because no scripture says the

Holy Spirit is given automatically when a person decides to convert to the way of the LORD. We are only talking about scriptural evidence and not theory or vain philosophy. There is a way a believer knows they have received the baptism of the Holy Spirit. It is not a question or debate whether a person can be born again with or without the Holy Spirit. It is clearly understood that a person cannot be a believer without the Holy Spirit based on the text of Romans 8:9, which says, "But ye are not in the flesh, but in the Spirit, if so be that the Spirit of God dwells in you. Now if any man have not the Spirit of Christ, he is none of his (KJV)." This is clear that a believer needs the Holy Spirit to be considered the possession of God as a child and heir to God's inheritance, so the debate is more about how we know a person has received the Holy Spirit. Romans 8:9 is also a clear contradiction to people who believe in the doctrine or teachings of what is considered the "fatherhood of God," which illudes that everyone who is ever born into this world is a child of God. To drive the point further, John 8:44 quotes JESUS to say, "Ye are of your father the devil," so therefore, GOD cannot be the father of everyone. A person must do the will of GOD to be considered a child. This is why the doctrine of the "Fatherhood of God" is deceiving people, and those who teach it are deceived themselves. Some will also call this the inclusive gospel.

What Happens When a Believer Receives the Holy Spirit

In Joel 2:28, God states, "And it shall come to pass afterward, that I will pour out my spirit upon all flesh; and your sons and your daughters shall prophesy, your old men shall dream dreams, your young men shall see visions: (KJV)." The first description of this text being fulfilled in the New Testament is in Acts 2:16, where it says, "But this is that which was spoken by the prophet Joel (KJV)." Acts 2:16 describes preceding events in the previous verses 3 and 4 stating,

> *"And there appeared unto them cloven tongues like as of fire, and it sat upon each of them. And they were all filled with the Holy Ghost, and **began to speak with other tongues**, as the Spirit gave them utterance (KJV)."*

It is clear that when the Holy Spirit filled the disciples of Christ, they "began to speak with other tongues," tongues meaning languages. The argument from some theologians is that the speaking of tongues in Acts chapter two was not a sign of receiving the Holy Spirit because it was the Holy Spirit that allowed them to speak known languages of the Jews from other regions that came to Jerusalem for the feast of Pentecost so they can hear and understand the message of God and the tongues in modern Christian churches is not legible languages. This is partially true; however, this does not discount the fact that speaking in other tongues was what happened to the disciples after receiving the Holy Spirit. The only truth to this argument is that other Jews heard them speak known legible languages. Therefore, many argue that tongues are only to understand the message of GOD if there is no translator. This would contradict Paul's message to the Corinthian church in 1 Corinthians chapter 14 as he described tongues as a language nobody understands and is meant to speak to GOD and have a personal edification. The New Living Translation puts it into context as it says, "For if you have the ability to speak in tongues, you will be talking only to God since people won't be able to understand you. You will speak by the power of the Spirit, but it will all be mysterious. But one who prophesies strengthens others, encourages them, and comforts them. A person who speaks in tongues is strengthened personally, but one who speaks a word of prophecy strengthens the entire church (1 Corinthians 14:2-4 NLT)." Another point is that the Jews who heard their languages did not hear a message from God but only acknowledged that they heard them speaking in their language, and other Jews mocked them and accused them of being drunk, which shows that they were speaking incoherently. It was not until Peter began speaking in a common language for all to understand and declared to them what was happening and said that it was the fulfillment of the prophecy of Joel 2:28.

    Joel 2:28 was not the only scripture that foretold the ability to speak with tongues because Mark 16:17-18 states, "17 And these signs shall follow them that believe; In my name shall they cast out devils; **they shall speak with new tongues**; They shall take up serpents; and if they drink any deadly thing, it shall not hurt them; they shall lay hands on the sick, and they shall recover (KJV)." This text leads us to the events in Acts chapter 2, verse four, which is not the only text that describes believers speaking in tongues after receiving the Holy Spirit. Acts chapter two describes the Jews receiving the Holy Spirit. The next text that describes the phenomenon of glossolalia is in Acts 10:44-46.

> *While Peter yet spake these words, the Holy Ghost fell on all them which heard the word. And they of the circumcision which believed were astonished, as many as came with Peter, because that on the Gentiles also was poured out the gift of the Holy Ghost.* **For they heard them speak with tongues**, *and magnify God (Acts 10: 44-46 KJV)."*

The next text is found in Acts chapter 19:

> *2 He said unto them, Have ye received the Holy Ghost since ye believed? And they said unto him, We have not so much as heard whether there be any Holy Ghost. 6 And when Paul had laid his hands upon them, the Holy Ghost came on them; and* **they spake with tongues**, *and prophesied (Acts 19:2,6 KJV).*

The reason why these three texts in Acts 2:4, Acts 10:44-46, and Acts 19:2,6 are important is that it is coming from the book of Acts, which is the historical book of the New Testament to instruct believers of how the church began and how to carry it forward. It is the book that offers complete instructions on New Testament salvation, and the remainder of the books of the New Testament teach how to live victoriously in Christ JESUS. It established the Law of First Mention, and after the book of Acts, there were letters to either church that were established and to pastors and then the book of Revelations.

Based on scriptural evidence speaking in tongues were the experience that the Jews received in Acts chapter two, it was the experience that the Gentiles received in Acts chapter 10, and it was the experience that those who already believed and were serving received in Acts chapter nineteen. This is not to say that speaking in tongues is the Holy Spirit, this is to say that speaking in tongues happens when a believer receives the Holy Spirit as a sign that they entered into covenant with GOD.

Fruit of the Spirit Argument

Another argument is that the sign or proof that you received the Holy Spirit is found in the book of Galatians 5:22-23 where it states, "But the fruit of the Spirit is love, joy, peace, longsuffering, gentleness, goodness, faith, Meekness, temperance: against such there is no law (KJV)." This does show characteristics that a believer who has the Holy Spirit should be displaying, however, this does not teach that this is what happens upon receiving the Holy Spirit. This is a teaching about the contrast between the works of the flesh and the works of the Spirit. You need the Holy Spirit to be able to exemplify these characteristics. Let us look at the text in context:

19 Now the **works of the flesh** *are manifest, which are these; Adultery, fornication, uncleanness, lasciviousness, 20 Idolatry, witchcraft, hatred, variance, emulations, wrath, strife, seditions, heresies, 21 Envyings, murders, drunkenness, revellings, and such like: of the which I tell you before, as I have also told you in time past, that they which do such things shall not inherit the kingdom of God. 22* **But the fruit of the Spirit** *is love,* *joy, peace, longsuffering, gentleness, goodness, faith, 23 Meekness, temperance: against such there is no law (Galatians 5: 19-23, KJV).*

You only get fruit from a seed, and therefore, a person must already have the Holy Spirit for it to produce fruit. If the fruit of the spirit is the initial evidence that a person has received the baptism of the Holy Spirit, then it would be reiterated more than once and would have been included as the evidence in the book of Acts, which is the history of the birth of the church. On the day of Pentecost, it did not say when the Holy Spirit sat upon them; they began to display the fruit of the spirit. It said they began to speak with other tongues, and that process was repeated in the book of Acts.

There must be proof that a person has received the Holy Spirit that is clear to the believer to show they received this great gift. At the beginning of the chapter, I used the text Acts 19:2

> *He said unto them, Have ye received the Holy Ghost since ye believed? (Acts 19:2 KJV)*

This text illudes that there must be some evidence beyond believing or receiving Christ as the LORD and Savior because the main character of Acts chapter 19 is Apollos, who was described as a powerful minister preaching Christ. The scriptures testify of him:

> *"And a certain Jew named Apollos, born at Alexandria, **an eloquent man**, and **mighty in the scriptures**, came to Ephesus. This man was **instructed in the way of the Lord**; and being*

> *fervent in the spirit, he spake and taught diligently the things of the Lord*, knowing only the baptism of John. And he began to **speak boldly in the synagogue**: whom when Aquila and Priscilla had heard, they took him unto them, and expounded unto him the way of God more perfectly. And when he was disposed to pass into Achaia, the brethren wrote, exhorting the disciples to receive him: who, when he was come, helped them much which had believed through grace: For **he mightily convinced the Jews, and that publicly, shewing by the scriptures that Jesus was Christ** (Acts 8:24-28, KJV)."

This text not only highlights a person who was more versed and influential than most preachers of any time in history but also the quality that he possessed that preachers today do not have: the humility to continue to learn. He obviously was not threatened by Paul asking to have received the Holy Spirit since he believed but inquired about it, and his way of baptism was also questioned. If this happened to believers today who are far less than Apollos, their response would be to take offense because of all that they have accomplished and would be upset that someone would question their salvation or understanding of the scriptures. Apollos is the perfect example of a believer, and not only that but a preacher who is humble enough and convicted in his belief that he would listen to others that could aid him in understanding the will of GOD more deeply. If his ministry was powerful before receiving the correct baptism in water and the baptism of the Holy Spirit had to enhance it further.

Tongues have Ceased Argument

In my time in ministry, I have met and discussed many beliefs about the Holy Spirit, and one of the arguments that makes the least sense is that speaking in tongues has ceased and was only for the first-century church. The scripture that most people use that believe this is 1 Corinthians 13:8, says, "Charity never faileth: but whether there be prophecies, they shall fail; whether there be tongues, they shall cease; whether there be knowledge, it shall vanish away (KJV)." People who adhere to this argument use this scripture out of context, and furthermore, you need more than one scripture to support a sound interpretation. Let us examine this text. Paul's subject was about the important of love above anything else in the body of Christ because he opens the text about his ability to be able to speak with the tongues of angels. His point was that no matter the believer's ability, the most important thing is to have love. Verse 8 does not say that tongues have ceased, but it talks about the time when all believers have made it to that new earth and city of Jerusalem, that the church age will be over, and there will be no more need for speaking in tongues or prophecies, or knowledge. That is not for this current time because if there are no more tongues, then there are no more prophecies or knowledge, and therefore, we all cannot hear from GOD, and we are all ignorant because we cannot understand the knowledge of GOD. This is why it is so important to read the whole scripture to get context and not to cherry-pick one phrase to support why you do not believe in a certain teaching. Tongues have not ceased because it was given to the church as a way to communicate with GOD and strengthen and build up the saint according to 1 Corinthians 14:2-4 *For he that speaketh in an unknown tongue speaketh not unto men, but unto God: for no man understandeth him; howbeit in the spirit he speaketh mysteries. But he that prophesieth speaketh unto men to edification, and exhortation, and comfort. He that speaketh in an unknown tongue edifieth himself; but he that prophesieth edifieth the church (KJV).* GOD has not taken or caused tongues to cease, as it plays a vital role in the believer's spiritual journey.

As mentioned at the beginning of the chapter, we wanted to discuss what happens when a believer is baptized in the Holy Spirit. Below is the discussion on why a believer receives the Holy Spirit and how important it is to the New Testament church.

Holy Spirit as a Sign of Covenant with God

There is nowhere in the Bible where God considered everyone his child because he clearly distinguishes between the world and those in covenant with him. The key word is covenant because the Holy Spirit baptism is a sign of the LORD's covenant with his people to identify them as children of God. 2 Corinthians 3:6 states, He has given us the power to serve under a new covenant. The covenant is not based on the written Law of Moses. It comes from the Holy Spirit. The written Law kills, but the Spirit gives life (NIRV). When God establishes a covenant with people, it always comes with a sign or ratification where the sign becomes a symbol of making it official. For example, when God destroyed the earth with the flood, and he promised he would not destroy the earth with water again, he made a covenant with Noah, and the sign of the covenant was the rainbow according to Genesis

9:15-16, stating, "And I will remember my covenant, which is between me and you and every living creature of all flesh; and the waters shall no more become a flood to destroy all flesh. And the bow shall be in the cloud; and I will look upon it, that I may remember the everlasting covenant between God and every living creature of all flesh that is upon the earth (KJV)." When God was making a covenant with Abraham in the book of Genesis in chapters 12, 13, 17, and 22, the summation of it was to make a great nation out of him, bless him, make his name great, bless his people with land, bless whoever bless him, and cause his people to be a great number to where they can't be numbered. The blessings were contingent upon Abraham and his people to obey his voice. However, the sign of the covenant was described in Genesis 17:10-11 as circumcision, "This is my covenant, which ye shall keep, between me and you and thy seed after thee; Every man child among you shall be circumcised. And ye shall circumcise the flesh of your foreskin, and it shall be a token of the covenant betwixt me and you (KJV)." Some would describe this as two separate covenants, Abrahamic and Palestinian, but they are one of the same. The next covenant is what is considered the Mosaic covenant, which used Moses to lead his people out of bondage in Egypt and bring them to the land that he promised to Abraham and the covenant he made with them was conditional upon them keeping his commandments as described as the ten commandments in Exodus chapter 20 but expounded in the book of Leviticus. The sign of his covenant made to Israel in the wilderness was the Sabbath. In Exodus 31:16-17 states, "Wherefore the children of Israel shall keep the sabbath, to observe the sabbath throughout their generations, for a perpetual covenant. It is a sign between me and the children of Israel for ever: for in six days the Lord made heaven and earth, and on the seventh day he rested, and was refreshed (KJV)." And when it comes to the New Testament or Covenant church, the Holy Spirit is what seals a believer into the body of Christ according to Ephesians 1:13, saying, "ye were sealed with that holy Spirit of promise (KJV)." However, in Romans 2:29 the Holy Spirit is compared to the Abrahamic covenant sign of circumcision by saying, "but someone is a Jew who is one inwardly, and circumcision is of the heart by the Spirit and not by the written code. This person's praise is not from people but from God (NET)."

1. The Holy Spirit as a Promise
    a. Joel 2:28 And it shall come to pass afterward, that I will pour out my spirit upon all flesh; and your sons and your daughters shall prophesy, your old men shall dream dreams, your young men shall see visions: (KJV)
    b. O.T. the Lord gave individuals the Spirit for certain purposes.
    c. N.T. the Lord gives every believer the Holy Spirit to carry out his work together.
2. The Holy Spirit as the Seal of God
    a. Ephesians 1:13 In whom ye also trusted, after that ye heard the word of truth, the gospel of your salvation:

in whom also after that ye believed, ye were sealed with that holy Spirit of promise, (KJV)
   b. you were marked with the seal of the promised Holy Spirit, (Eph 1:13, NET)
   c. 2 Corinthians 1:22 Who hath also sealed us and given the earnest of the Spirit in our hearts. (KJV)
   d. 2 Corinthians 1:22 who also sealed us and gave us the Spirit in our hearts as a down payment. (NET)
   e. This is a metaphor taken of a seal, which, being put on anything, distinguishes between those things that are authentic and those things that are not.
   f. Song of Solomon 8:6 Set me as a seal upon thine heart, as a seal upon thine arm: for love is strong as death; jealousy is cruel as the grave: the coals thereof are coals of fire, which hath a most vehement flame. (KJV)
   g. Isaiah 8:16 Bind up the testimony, seal the law among my disciples. (KJV)
3. The Work of the Holy Spirit
   a. Acts 1:8 – Gives Power
   b. Acts 2:39 – Promise
   c. Gal 5:22-23 – Produces Fruit
   d. John 16:13 – Guides into truth
   e. Romans 8:26 – Assist in Prayer
   f. John 14:26 – Teaches
   g. 2 Cor. 4:7 – Priceless

h. Romans 5:3 – Pleasure
i. 1 Cor. 12 – Gift Giver
j. Sanctifier
k. Romans 8:14 – Leader
l. Roman 8:9 - Bear witness of ownership

CHAPTER 12 TOUCH NOT MINE ANOINTED

Miseducation: *No one is allowed to correct or challenge a minister who pastors or preaches.*

> *1 Chronicles 16:22 Saying, Touch not mine anointed, and do my prophets no harm. (KJV)*

For many years, there have been people in the Body of Christ that has used 1 Chronicles 16:22 as scripture to pardon preachers of their immoral conduct or erroneous ways to say they are above reproach. Many Christians believe that no one should be allowed to say anything to or about preachers who have questionable behaviors. These are people "who loveth to have the preeminence (3 Jn 1:9, KJV)." When looking at 1 Chron. 16:22, it is not an excuse to leave the sins of preachers unchecked or without rebuke. To understand this scripture in context, it must be read in context from 1 Chronicles chapter 16 verses 19-22.

> *1 Chron. 16:19-22 When ye were but few, even a few, and strangers in it. And when they went from nation to nation, and from one kingdom to another people; He suffered no man to do them wrong: yea, he reproved kings for their sakes, Saying, Touch not mine anointed, and do my prophets no harm. (KJV)*

In Psalms 105:12-15 it mirrors 1 Chron. 16:19-22 to give clarity of the subject matter:

> *Ps 105:12-15 When they were but a few men in number; yea, very few, and strangers in it. When they went from one nation to another, from one kingdom to another people; He suffered no man to do them wrong: yea, he reproved kings for their sakes; Saying, Touch not mine anointed, and do my prophets no harm. (KJV)*

It is clear that in 1 Chronicles 16:22, God refers to Israel as being the Lord's anointed and his messengers (prophets) who were protected against the other nations that surrounded them. They were chosen as his people based on the Abrahamic Covenant, and as they were developing as a nation and being surrounded by foreign and pagan nations, God's hedge of protection was around.

Preachers who are living in a way that brings reproach to God are to be rebuked and reproved. There are many scriptures that address the intolerable acts of ministers that do not represent GOD's will. If 1 Chron. 16:22 could be used for preachers, then the question is why the apostle Paul would withstand Peter to his face in Gal. 2:11-14 and said he was the blame for the division between the Jew and Gentile believer. If we are not to touch the LORD's anointed then why would Jeremiah state, "the prophets prophesy falsely, and the priests bear rule by their means (Jeremiah 5:31, KJV)." If we are not to touch the LORD's anointed, then why would Hosea say, "the prophet is a fool and the spiritual man is mad (Hos. 9:7, KJV)."

Another scripture that is misused is KJV 1 Timothy 5:1, when it says, "Rebuke not an elder." This scripture does not convey to not rebuke a preacher, but it is instructions from Paul to Timothy as a young pastor how to use wisdom in dealing with the older saints and not to chastise them but to treat them as fathers and mothers. I remember being grieved one time when I heard a young, arrogant, or ignorant preacher tell me how he was disturbed when an older, seasoned saint tried to give him some advice that went against his grain, and he tried to use 1 Tim. 5:1 in his defense as to say she had no right correcting him because he was an elder. In his misinterpretation of the scripture, he did not understand that he should have listened with humility and respect because she was his elder, and he was supposed to treat her as a mother and not a subordinate.

Let us read another scripture that supports the rebuke of erroneous preachers. Romans 16:17,18 states:

> *Now I beseech you, brethren, mark them which cause divisions and offences contrary to the doctrine which ye have learned; and avoid them. For they that are such serve not our Lord Jesus Christ, but their own belly; and by good words and fair speeches deceive the hearts of the simple (KJV)*

Another scripture that is used in error about the subject at hand is:

> *1 Samuel 24:10. "Behold, this day thine eyes have seen how that the LORD had delivered thee today into mine hand in the cave: and some bade me kill thee: but mine eye spared thee; and I*

said, I will not put forth mine hand against my lord; for he is the LORD'S anointed (KJV)."

This verse tells the story of the conflict between King Saul and David his successor. Saul had pursued David to harm him and David found himself with the upper hand on Saul and did not have the heart to harm Saul even though he proclaimed that "the LORD had delivered" Saul into his hands. At this point in the narrative, Saul was not the Lord's anointed because GOD, through the prophet Samuel, had already anointed David for the throne but just had not ascended to the throne yet.

With so many erroneous teachings today, along with charlatans and false and foolish prophets, there needs to be a people who learn not to accept anything that comes over the pulpit without feeling the shame of preachers lashing out in defense as if they are above reproach. If there is no one who is willing to stand for truth, then there will be a great chance that "they be blind leaders of the blind. And if the blind lead the blind, both shall fall into the ditch (Matthew 15:14 KJV)." Furthermore, we are instructed to "believe not every spirit, but try the spirits whether they are of God: because many false prophets are gone out into the world (1 John 4:1 KJV)."

CHAPTER 13 WAS JESUS ABLE TO SIN OR ABLE NOT TO SIN?

Miseducation: JESUS was able to sin but chose not to do so to be an example for believers.

This chapter addresses the controversial question of whether Jesus had the ability to sin. Many teach Jesus could have sinned and chose not to and was our example of how to overcome temptation. I also have heard people say because he was a man he could have sinned. I want readers to examine the evidence of scripture for themselves and see why I take the position that it was impossible for Jesus to sin. There is an infatuation among men that attempts to attribute human characteristics to GOD. This is considered anthropomorphism and it is a mistake to take a holy GOD that is infinite and reduce HIM to humankind. Although JESUS was manifested in the flesh, HE was very much a deity as Paul said, "GOD was manifest into flesh (1 Timothy 3:16 KJV)." It is impossible for GOD to have the ability to sin because that would disqualify HIM from being GOD. GOD is holy, and if HE could sin, then that would make HIM a sinner because sin comes from the nature of man, and he was not man but GOD. This is why Paul states, "Let this mind be in you, which was also in Christ Jesus: (Philippians 2:5 KJV)." Sin starts in the inner man or the mind of a person and that is why JESUS could not have sinned because HIS mind or spirit is holy and of deity. A person's sin is conceived first in their mind according to James 1:15, "Then when desire conceives, it gives birth to sin, and when sin is full grown, it gives birth to death (NET)."

Old Testament Typology of the Sacrificial Lamb

> *Lev. 1:3 If his offering be a burnt sacrifice of the herd, let him offer a male without blemish: he shall offer it of his own voluntary will at the door of the tabernacle of the congregation before the Lord. (KJV)*

According to Leviticus 1:3, the sacrificial lamb must be without blemish. JESUS is typified as the sacrificial lamb of GOD to take away the sins of the world, and in order for HIM to be that sacrificial lamb, HE had to be without spot or blemish to be a valid sacrifice. This illudes the sin because in the Old Testament, the children of Israel would bring a sacrificial lamb without blemish, so the priest would pray the sins of the person or family that brings the lamb onto the lamb, and then the lamb would be sacrificed to symbolize the taking away of their sins. If the lamb had a blemish, then the lamb would not be worthy of sacrifice.

The sacrificial system in the Old Testament was a type and shadow for things to come. Jesus, as proclaimed by John as the lamb of GOD who came to take away the sins of the world (John 1:29 KJV)" had to be without blemish as the Old Testament sacrifice, or HE would not have qualified as the lamb of GOD. If we look at Jesus' sacrifice on the cross, we see that HE went through the same Old Testament custom of identification and examination of the lamb by the priest to see if there was any blemish. This is why the account of Luke 23:4 describes Pilate announcing, "to the chief priests and to the people, I find no fault in this man (KJV)." And then Pilate sent him to Herod, and when Herod examined him, he stated, "and unto them, Ye have brought this man unto me, as one that perverteth the people: and, behold, I, having examined him before you, have found no fault in this man touching those things whereof ye accuse him (Luke 23:14 KJV)." Even though this did not exonerate JESUS, this did prove before many witnesses that he was without spot or blemish and could be the sacrificial lamb of GOD. He then proceeded to the cross and was the scapegoat and the goat for atonement. He was wounded and died in isolation as the scapegoat, and his blood was shed for our atonement, and this can only be done by the high priest, so JESUS was also our high priest because he declared, "No man taketh it from me, but I lay it down of myself. I have power to lay it down, and I have power to take it again (John 10:18 KJV)."

So, in other words, there is no evidence in scripture that JESUS could have sinned if he wanted to because he was the lamb of GOD. Furthermore, the following scripture state:

1. 2 Cor. 5:21 For he hath made him to be sin for us**, who knew no sin**; that we might be made the righteousness of God in him.
2. 1 Pet. 2:22 **Who did no sin**, neither was guile found in his mouth:

3. 1 Jn. 3:5 And ye know that he was manifested to take away our sins; **and in him is no sin**.
4. Heb. 4:15 For we have not an high priest which cannot be touched with the feeling of our infirmities; but was in all points tempted like as we are, **yet without sin**.
5. Heb. 7:26 For such an high priest became us, who is holy, harmless, undefiled, **separate from sinners**, and made higher than the heavens;

We have JESUS who knew no sin, did no sin, in him is no sin, yet without sin, and HE was separate from sinners.

He did not have an Adamic Nature to Sin

Another point to make is that in order for JESUS to have the ability to sin he would have had to have an Adamic nature. The Adamic nature means that since all of the human race descends from Adam the first man, then the sin that Adam and Even committed in the garden was passed down through the human DNA or our human genetics that "all have sinned and come short of the glory of GOD (Romans 3:23 KJV)." JESUS did not have the Adamic nature, but his nature was the nature of GOD. Let us read 1 Corinthians 15:45-47:

---

45 and so it is written, The first man Adam was made a living soul; the last Adam was made a quickening spirit. 46 Howbeit that was not first which is spiritual, but that which is natural; and afterward that which is spiritual. 47 The first

> *man is of the earth, earthy; the second man is the Lord from heaven.(KJV)*

This text clearly makes a distinction between Adam and JESUS. JESUS is a quickening spirit, which means HE was a life-giving spirit as opposed to Adam, who was made a living person. In verse forty-seven it says that JESUS was the Lord from heaven, but Adam was from the earth made from dust. Since JESUS was the Lord from heaven, then the LORD cannot sin or have the ability to sin.

The argument that JESUS could sin because he was man like we are is also not supported by scripture because when the scripture describes JESUS as a man, it is speaking to his appearance as a man, but the scripture declares that JESUS came "in the **likeness** of sinful flesh (Rom 8:3 KJV)," "and took upon him the **form** of a servant, and was made in the **likeness** of men (Philippians 2:7 KJV)," "and being found in **fashion** as a man (Phil 2:8 KJV)." However, HE was not a man as we are but just was a likeness of man but "for in him all the fullness of deity lives in bodily form (Colossians 2:9 NET)."

CHAPTER 14 TRICHOTOMY VS. DICHOTOMY

The Relationship Between
the Heart, Soul, Mind, & Spirit

Genesis 2:7 And the LORD God formed man of the dust of the ground, and breathed into his nostrils the breath of life; and man became a living soul. (KJV)

Deuteronomy 6:5 And thou shalt love the LORD thy God with all thine heart, and with all thy soul, and with all thy might. (KJV; ref, Matt 22:37; Mk 12:30; Lk 10:27)

Hebrews 4:12 For the word of God is quick, and powerful, and sharper than any two-edged sword, piercing even to the dividing asunder of soul and spirit, and of the joints and marrow, and is a discerner of the thoughts and intents of the heart. (KJV)

The relationship between heart, soul, mind, and spirit can be difficult to distinguish because they are not clear distinctions but are a harmonious rhythm of our existence. From a Hebrew perspective, the human structure is a dichotomy that only categorizes the existence of our creation as body and soul, with the soul being synonymous with spirit, mind, and heart. However, there are scriptures, especially in the New Covenant, that discuss a trichotomy of our existence and make distinctions between the soul and spirit or soul and heart (i.e., 1 Thes 5:23 & Heb 4:12). One of the reasons that it is hard to tell if there are distinctions is because Hebrew scriptures have many parallels in it because of the poetic nature. A Hebrew parallel is a structure of thought in which the writer balances a series of words that have intentional repetition. For example, Isaiah 53:5 states, "he was wounded for our transgressions, he was bruised for our iniquities (KJV)." The words wounded and bruised have the same meaning but are worded differently, just as transgressions and iniquities are the same but worded differently. This could be true for the soul, spirit, heart, and mind. From a Hebrew perspective, these terms could be mentioned in the exact text but have a Hebrew parallel connotation to them.

A question was asked: Does the heart enfold the soul, or is the heart a part of the soul? Before asking this question, we must see how the Bible uses the terms heart, soul, mind, and spirit. We must also see how those terms are defined based on the languages of the Bible.

The first mention of the soul in the Bible is in Genesis 2:7 when it says, And the LORD God formed man of the dust of the ground and breathed into his nostrils the breath of life, and man became a living soul. (KJV)" In this text, the body was created first with all its organs and components, and the LORD ALMIGHTY activated that body by breathing into it. The term soul in this text comes from the Hebrew word (נֶפֶשׁ nephesh neh'-fesh), which is translated as a soul in the King James version, but in other translations, is translated as being or creature.

Nephesh (נֶפֶשׁ neh'-fesh) is defined as: soul, self, life, creature, person, appetite, mind, living being, desire, emotion, passion 1a) that which breaths, the breathing substance or being, soul, the inner being of man 1b) living being 1c) living being (with life in the blood) 1d) the man himself, self, person or individual 1e) seat of the appetites 1f) seat of emotions and passions 1g) activity of mind 1g1) dubious 1h) activity of the will 1h1) dubious 1i) activity of the character 1i1) dubious.

This Hebrew word has been translated as soul 475 times, life 117, person 29, mind 15, heart 15, creature 9, body 8, himself 8, yourselves 6, dead 5, will 4, desire 4, man 3, themselves 3, and 3, appetite 2, and 45 times miscellaneous. With this in mind, we can already see that at times in the scripture soul, mind, and heart can be synonymous, but this is not always the case.

In the book of Deuteronomy 6:5, it says, "And thou shalt love the LORD thy God with all thine heart, and with all thy soul, and with all thy might (KJV)." The reference texts to Deut. 6:5 is: Matt 22:37; Mk 12:30; Lk 10:27). In Deut. 6:5, the words heart and soul are in the exact text, and when reading its New Testament reiterations, soul and heart are mentioned as well as mind. I believe that by the New Testament texts, renderings of Deuteronomy 6:5, adding the word mind gives a persuasive case for Hebrew parallelism and repetitively using words that mean the same thing to put emphasis that the LORD ALMIGHTY wants our total being to be engulfed with love for Him. The reason is that καρδία kardia usage in the N.T. is translated as the heart (102), heart's (1), hearts (49), mind (2), minds (1), quick (1), spirit (1). ψυχή psuche is translated as the heart (2), heartily (1), life (36), lives (7), mind

(1), minds (1), the person (1), persons (3), soul (33), souls (14), suspense*(1), thing (1). διάνοια dianoia is translated as mind (7), minds (2), thoughts (1), and understanding (2). With all three words having the ability to be translated as mind, then the Hebrew parallelism makes sense that this is the word for emphasis.

The only text in the Bible that has soul, spirit, and heart in it simultaneously is Hebrew 4:12 which states, "For the word of God is quick, and powerful, and sharper than any two-edged sword, piercing even to the dividing asunder of soul and spirit, and of the joints and marrow, and is a discerner of the thoughts and intents of the heart."(KJV) This text seems to make a strong case for a distinction between the soul and the spirit because it states that they can be divided. However, it is plausible to view the soul here as creation and the spirit as the life force, and if they are divided, then life will cease to exist as a person. This still puts us into a dichotomy view of the text as in body and soul or body and spirit. In Ecclesiastes 12:7 it says, "Then shall the dust return to the earth as it was: and the spirit shall return unto God who gave it. (KJV)" Spirit here is likely referent is the life's breath that originates with God in Gen 2:7, but in Gen 2:7, it is called soul. The spirit is considered the breath, and without breathing, the body cannot survive. God breathed the breath of life into Adam, which made him a living soul (creature/being), and the word spirit means exactly what God did.

πνεῦμα pneuma {pnyoo'-mah} is defined as a movement of air (a gentle blast) of the wind, hence the wind itself; the breath of nostrils or mouth; the spirit, i.e., the vital principal by which the body is animated; the rational spirit, the power by which the human being feels, thinks, decides.

Since the words soul, spirit, heart, and mind can be used interchangeably at times, it is safe to say that they all keep the body mobile, and without one, you cannot have the other. You cannot have a spirit without having a soul, and you cannot have a soul without having a heart. The soul is the entire being of a person, and the spirit, heart, and mind are the intelligence, emotional state, and personality of the soul.

Furthermore, we can simply look at the lexical definition of spirit to determine its full semantic range and understand that spirit is considered the same as soul, mind, and heart.

CHAPTER 15 DOES GOD EVER CHANGE HIS MIND?

Miseducation: God can change his mind in certain situations if he prefers to because he's God.

There are two views when it comes to the teaching of whether GOD can change his mind or not. One is what is considered the Liberal View or Open Theism which means that GOD can change his mind anytime HE feels necessary. The scripture that is used by the proponents of the Liberal View is Exodus 32:14:

> *Exodus 32:14 And the Lord repented of the evil which he thought to do unto his people. KJV*

The second view of the teaching of whether GOD can change HIS mind is the Traditional View which means that GOD cannot change his mind. The scripture that is used by the proponents of the Traditional View is Malachi 3:6:

> *Malachi 3:6 For I am the Lord, **I change not**; therefore ye sons of Jacob are not consumed. KJV*

It is hard to believe that GOD changes his mind when Malachi 3:6 is emphatic that GOD does not change under any circumstances. Furthermore, Numbers 23:19 states, "God is not a man, that he should lie; **neither the son of man, that he should repent**: hath he said, and shall he not do it? or hath he spoken, and shall he not make it good (KJV)?" In the NET translation, it reads as such: "God is not a man, that he should lie, **nor a human being, that he should change his mind**. Has he said, and will he not do it? Or has he spoken, and will he not make it happen (Number 23:19 NET)?" When any scripture say that GOD repented then it is not as man repents or change because GOD does not change. Another text is Hebrew 13:8 where it says, "**Jesus Christ is the same yesterday and today and forever** (KJV)!" Through this chapter we will show how GOD does not change or repent as meaning change but is nothing more than a misunderstanding and interpretation of the text.

To analyze this subject, we must examine the scriptures that most people use to support their theory that God changes his mind.

We will start with Exodus 32:14, in which the King James Version translates the text as GOD repented of the evil. In Exodus 32:14, the Hebrew word for repent is " נחם (nacham)" which is a passive verb that means to be sorry and console oneself. According to the Brow-Driver-Briggs Hebrew English Lexicon this verb in Exodus 32:14 means to be sorry, moved to pity, have compassion for others."[1] It does not mean that GOD changed his mind. It simply means that GOD saw what happened to Israel due to his judgment, and he felt pity on them. This is no different than a loving parent that must punish his child so the child can learn from their mistakes, however, the parent feels remorse because of the love they have for the child. The verb that indicates the action is in the passive voice called a *Niphal* in Hebrew, and therefore, it is an action that had already happened to Israel, and the result of the action caused GOD to be moved with pity. Another scripture that contains the Hebrew *Niphal* verb is in the Genesis record in chapter six. Gen. 6:6 says, "And it repented the Lord that he had made man on the earth, and it grieved him at his heart (KJV)." The word repent in this text is the same Hebrew verb "וַיִּנָּחֶם (nacham)" as in Exodus 32:14. It is better understood in this verse as regret as the NET translation presents: Gen. 6:6 "The Lord regretted that he had made humankind on the earth, and he was highly offended (NET)."

There are two Hebrew words that most people often confuse the meaning of "וַיִּנָּחֶם (nacham)" "שׁוּב shuwb." These Hebrew words are not to be confused with the Greek word "μετανοέω metanoeō" nor is it equivalent. Metanoeō means to change one's mind, i.e., to repent; to change one's mind for better, heartily to amend with abhorrence of one's past sins. This is an action that humankind performs when they are not only sorrowful for their wrong deeds but are willing to turn away from their sinful ways and turn to GOD. This is not the idea of repenting when it some scriptures translate the Hebrew words nacham and shuwb into the word repent or repentance to describe GOD's action.

The word **nacham** is defined as to be sorry, console oneself, repent, regret, comfort, be comforted; a. (Niphal) to be sorry, be moved to pity, have compassion; 2) to be sorry, rue, suffer grief, repent; 3) to comfort oneself, be comforted; 4) to comfort oneself, ease oneself; b. (Piel) to comfort, console; c. (Pual) to be comforted, be consoled; c. (Hithpael) 1) to be sorry, have compassion; 2) to rue, repent of 3) to comfort oneself, be comforted; 4) to ease oneself.

The word **shuwb** is defined as: 1) to return, turn back; a) (Qal) 1) to turn back, return; b) (Polel) 1) to bring back; c) (Pual) restored (participle); d) (Hiphil) to cause to return, bring back; 1) to bring back, allow to return, put back, draw back, give back, restore, relinquish, give in payment; e) (Hophal) to be returned, be restored, be brought back; f) (Pulal) brought back. Shuwb is also a root in the word **Teshuvah** which means: 1) admit the wrong to self and the one wronged with sincere regret 2) make amends and ameliorate damage as best one can with restitution 3) A sincere vow before God to never commit the same act (a return from wrongdoing) but also to relent: a) to become less severe, harsh, or strict usually from reasons of humanity. b) let up, slacken.

In simple terms, nacham means to be sorry and to console oneself, shuwb means to turn back and to return, and teshuvah means to return. If there is any correlation between "metanoeō" to one of these Hebrew terms, it would be "teshuvah" because we are called to turn back to GOD.

Another problem that occurs when thinking in terms that GOD changes His mind is the doctrine of perfect will and permissive will of GOD. The scripture never mentions that GOD has a permissive will. I have heard preachers use this term to say that when a person does not follow GOD's perfect will for them, then GOD will have a permissive will. This defies the very meaning of the word "will." The "will" of GOD simply means his desire, so GOD has a desire for all mankind and it is mentioned in 2 Peter 3:9, "The Lord is not slack concerning his promise, as some men count slackness; but is longsuffering to us-ward, **not willing that any should perish, but that all should come to repentance** (KJV)." Also, Romans 12:2 says, "And be not conformed to this world: but be ye transformed by the renewing of your mind, that ye may prove what is that good, and acceptable, and **perfect, will of God** (KJV)." GOD's way and His will is always perfect, according to Psalm 18:30 and 2 Samuel 22:32, and it is never permissive. A person is either in GOD's will or not. If a person is not in GOD's will, then GOD is just having mercy on them, and it is not a permissive will, or an alternative desire or contingency plan GOD has for that person.

In the Torah, repentance is an active process. To regret the action that was done by itself without changing your way or making amends is not considered an act of repentance. Nicham is to feel regret or sorrow and "shuv" is to return. When a person wrongs another person in any way that causes harm, whether it is physical or emotional, and is unfaithful to the ALMIGHTY GOD, then that person is guilty and must confess the sin that has been committed. He must make full restitution for his wrong, add one-fifth to it, and give it all to the person he has wronged. As in Numbers 5:6-7 and 30:8, "You will repent and obey God, keeping all His commandments, as I prescribe them to you today." Deuteronomy 30:8 note the Hebrew word tashuv, where teshuvah is the NOUN for repent I gave you right out of Torah a commandment to repent, and the word used is tashuv; nicham is a feeling of sorrowfulness and regretfulness for the wrong deed is only one step. You have not repented if all you have done is feel bad about something you did in the past. 2 Corinthians 7:10 "For godly sorrow worketh repentance to salvation not to be repented of: but the sorrow of the world worketh death (KJV)." According to the Torah, there is a three-step formula for "repentance" (teshuva = returning to G-d by returning to the proper path). Quoting from Mishneh Torah by the Rambam (Maimonides):

Rethinking the Text

I will now list scriptures that have interpreted the Hebrew word nacham as repent, where many have misunderstood the idea that GOD can change his mind and following that scripture, put the same scripture in the NET translation, which gives it more context in conveying what is meant.

Psalm 106:45 (KJV) And he remembered for them his covenant, and **repented** according to the multitude of his mercies.

Psalm 106:45 (NET) He remembered his covenant with them, and **relented** because of his great loyal love.

Psalm 106:45 (KJV) And he remembered for them his covenant, and **repented** according to the multitude of his mercies.

Psalm 106:45 (NET) He remembered his covenant with them, and **relented** because of his great loyal love.

Jeremiah 18:8 (KJV) If that nation, against whom I have pronounced, turn from their evil, I will **repent** of the evil that I thought to do unto them.

Jeremiah 18:8 (NASB) if that nation against which I have spoken turns from its evil, I will **relent** of the disaster that I planned to bring on it.

Amos 7:3 (KJV) The Lord **repented** for this: It shall not be, saith the Lord.

Amos 7:3 (NASB) The Lord **relented** of this. "It shall not be," said the Lord.

Jeremiah 42:10 (KJV) If ye will still abide in this land, then will I build you, and not pull you down, and I will plant you, and not pluck you up: for I **repent** me of the evil that I have done unto you.

Jeremiah 42:10 (NET) For I am **filled with sorrow** because of the disaster that I have brought on you.

Jonah 3:9 (KJV) Who can tell if God will turn and **repent**, and turn away from his fierce anger, that we perish not?

Jonah 3:9 (NASB), (NIV) Who knows, God may turn and **relent** and withdraw His burning anger so that we will not perish."

Numbers 23:19 (KJV) God is not a man, that he should lie; neither the son of man, that he should **repent**: hath he said, and shall he not do it? Or hath he spoken, and shall he not make it good?

These scriptures show that depending on the translation is rendered the word "nacham" for repent that is translated into the King James Version could easily be understood or translated as relent, to be sorry, console oneself, regret, comfort, to be sorry, be moved to pity, have compassion; console; to ease oneself and if it is rendered as repent it is not with the thought that GOD can change his mind. In other words, "to say that God sometimes repents (e.g., 1 Samuel 15:11, 1 Samuel 15:35) and sometimes does not (1 Samuel 15:29) would be to argue that He sometimes can lie. In the same sense as with 'repent,' sometimes He does and sometimes He does not is ridiculous. But the truth is that God never lies, and so it requires the believe that He also never changes His mind."

Scriptures that Demonstrate that GOD Does not Change

Numbers 23:19 (NET) God is not a man, that he should lie, nor a human being, that he should change his mind. Has he said, and will he not do it? Or has he spoken, and will he not make it happen?

1 Samuel 15:29 (KJV) And also the Strength of Israel **will not lie nor repent**: for he is not a man, that he should repent.

1 Samuel 15:29 (NET) The Preeminent One of Israel **does not go back on his word or change his mind**, for he is not a human being who changes his mind."

Malachi 3:6 (KJV) For I am the Lord, **I change not**; therefore ye sons of Jacob are not consumed.

Malachi 3:6 (NET) Since, I, the Lord, **do not go back on my promises**, you, sons of Jacob, have not perished.

Scriptures that Translate Nacham and Shuwb in Other Terms

Gen 5:29 And he called his name Noah, saying, This same shall **comfort** (nacham H5162) us concerning our work and toil of our hands, because of the ground which the LORD hath cursed.

Gen 24:67 And Isaac brought her into his mother Sarah's tent, and took Rebekah, and she became his wife; and he loved her: and Isaac was **comforted** (nacham H5162) after his mother's death.

Gen 15:16 But in the fourth generation they shall **come hither again**: (shuwb H7725) for the iniquity of the Amorites is not yet full.

Gen 18:10 And he said, I will **certainly** (shuwb H7725) **return** (shuwb H7725) unto thee according to the time of life; and, lo, Sarah thy wife shall have a son. And Sarah heard it in the tent door, which was behind him.

Gen 18:33 And the LORD went his way, as soon as he had left communing with Abraham: and Abraham **returned** (shuwb H7725) unto his place.

Gen 20:7 Now therefore **restore** (shuwb H7725) the man his wife; for he is a prophet, and he shall pray for thee, and thou shalt live: and if thou **restore** (shuwb H7725) her not, know thou that thou shalt surely die, thou, and all that are thine.

In conclusion, Jesus Christ is the same yesterday, and today, and forever (Heb 13:8, KJV), and there is no variation or the slightest hint of change (James 1:17, NET).

CHAPTER 16 ETERNAL SECURITY & PREDESTINATION DEBATE

Miseducation: The Christian believer is predestined to salvation, and it is nothing they can do to void their route to glory.

For whom he did foreknow, he also did predestinate to be conformed to the image of his Son, that he might be the firstborn among many brethren. Moreover whom he did predestinate, them he also called: and whom he called, them he also justified: and whom he justified, them he also glorified. (Romans 8:29-30 KJV)

The subject of eternal security has been a long-debated subject among professing believers. We must first establish that there is no mention of the term or phrase "eternal security," but there are scriptures that seem to allude to the notion. However, it is read into it with the help of ignoring many other scriptures that instruct Christian believers to endure to the end and avoid worldly lust. If a believer is eternally secure, then this will leave the entire New Testament useless because no matter what we do, we are eternally secure. The other danger of believing this doctrine is that eternal security leads to erroneous teachings of predestination where many believe that they were chosen to be a part of GOD's glorious plan of salvation. This is an obstacle for sure because predestination would exclude many people, and therefore, GOD is partial. How can this be when the scripture clearly says, "For there is no partiality with God (Rom 2:11, KJV)."

One of the major proponents of eternal security was Augustine and John Calvin with his invention of the TULIP, which is an acronym for total depravity, unconditional election, limited atonement, irresistible grace, and perseverance of the saints. Augustine felt that the perseverance of the saints was a gift from GOD to all who believed and that no one can be separated from GOD. John Calvin took it further to say that the election of GOD was unconditional and that the grace of GOD was irresistible by the chosen.

There are too many scriptures to be ignored for eternal security to be valid. I remember there was a person who challenged me on conditional security by using only one scripture that came from John 18:9, saying, "That the saying might be fulfilled, which he spake, Of them, which thou gavest me have I lost none (KJV)." This is the example I quite often give of cherry-picking scripture to support a person's proposition. This scripture is not talking about all believers in Christ JESUS. This is talking about the apostles of the lamb. I say this because John 17:12 states, "12 While I was with them in the world, I kept them in thy name: those that thou gavest me I have kept, and none of them is lost, but the son of perdition; that the scripture might be fulfilled (KJV)." It clarifies that the ones that he has not lost were the twelve apostles except for the one Judas, who is considered to be the son of perdition.

Another scripture that follows the tenets of John Calvin would use is Romans 5:20: "Moreover the law entered, that the offence might abound. But where sin abounded, grace did much more abound: (KJV)." The interpretation of Romans 5:20 has been understood that if a believer has sinned then no matter how great the sin, grace would rise to the extent of the sin to cover it. It is true that if a believer sins, they can "confess our sins, he is faithful and just to forgive us our sins, and to cleanse us from all unrighteousness (1 Jn 1:9, KJV)." However, Romans 5:20 usage of a license to sin is incorrect, and it is presumptuous to think their sinful acts as grace would continue to cover it. This belief is known as antinomianism, which means that since Christians could be saved by grace, they can live however they want to live because of grace. This a strict contradiction to Romans 6:1, which says, "What shall we say then? Shall we continue in sin, that grace may abound (KJV)?" The book of Jude discusses how there were evil men who sneaked into the church and were turning the grace of our God into lasciviousness (1:4). This means using grace as a license to sin. Even the Psalmist in 19:13 prayed, "keep back thy servant also from presumptuous sins (KJV)."

Before we go too far, let us revisit the initial scripture at the beginning of the chapter that is the biggest stumbling block for those who adhere to eternal security, and that is Romans 8:29-30. There are certain terms that are associated with the eternal security debate, and they are foreknowledge, predestination, and election. These words have become hard to understand especially when opposed to free will.

Definitions

Foreknowledge is defined as to have knowledge beforehand, 2) to foreknow 2a) of those whom God elected to salvation, and 3) to predestinate. Predestination is defined as 1) to predetermine, decide beforehand, 2) in the NT of God decreeing from eternity, and 3) to foreordain, appoint beforehand. Election is defined as the act of picking out, and choosing 1a) the act of God's free will by which before the foundation of the world he decreed his blessings to certain persons 1b) the decree made from choice by which he determined to bless certain persons through Christ by grace alone 2) a thing or person chosen 2a) of persons: God's elect.

Let us take a look at foreknowledge first. Foreknowledge, in simple terms, means to know something ahead of time. The problem with using this term when it comes to individuals is dangerous and puts GOD as the dictator of all things that happen, both good and tragic. This is why so many believers stop having faith in GOD because they don't understand why a loving GOD would let tragedy happen if he knew it was going to happen and then to further add injury to insult, someone tries to comfort a person with words that it was GOD's will to let a person go through the torment of that tragedy. This is a subject that I will deal with in the next volume; however, in light of Romans 8:29-30, those he foreknew were not in an individual context. Many believe in the individual meaning of foreknowledge because Jeremiah 1:5 says, "Before I formed thee in the belly I knew thee; and before thou camest forth out of the womb I sanctified thee, and I ordained thee a prophet unto the nations (KJV)." This is personal to Jeremiah but many use it as a text that applies to everyone. Whatever the purpose GOD had for Jeremiah, who was the son of Hilkiah, the priest was one that was specific to Jeremiah. This scripture does not mean that GOD has ordained all of us before we are formed in our mother's womb. On the contrary, Romans 8:28-30 speaks of the church as the body of believers who he foreknew and not individuals. The pronoun "them" is illuding the Body of Christ that he knew as his ultimate hidden plan before the foundation of the earth. He predestined a plan that would allow anyone who believed to be a part of this glorious assembly.

John 3:16 states, For God so loved the world, that he gave his only begotten Son, that whosoever believeth in him should not perish, but have everlasting life (KJV)." Whosoever is speaking to the free will of man that if that person chooses to believe in JESUS, then that person has a chance to have everlasting life. This is also true of John 1:12 when it says, "But as many as received him, to them gave he power to become the sons of God, even to them that believe on his name (KJV)." JESUS died for the sins of the world as the lamb of God as John mentioned in John 1:29 that the lamb came to take away the sins of the world. If the lamb came to take away the sins of the world it means everyone and not certain individuals through GOD's predestined foreknowledge. GOD would not be a just god if he limits his salvation only to a certain group of people. In this case, there is no need to fulfill His commission and preach the gospel to every creature. The belief of the idea of a "personal savior" makes people feel good because of their belief that JESUS knew them before they came into the world and knew every sin they committed at the time JESUS went to the cross. People take this to mean that He died as their personal savior. This thinking is a product of foreknowledge and predestination because JESUS did not have to die for our individual personal sins. He died for the "sins of the world," and that included all kinds of sins that would ever be committed because as Solomon said, there is no new thing under the sun (Eccl 1:9, KJV)."

We cannot confuse foreknowledge and predestination with election. Foreknowledge has to do with GOD's plan and not individuals. For example, 1 Peter 1:20 states, "Who verily was **foreordained** before the foundation of the world, but was manifest in these last times for you (KJV)." This means that God had a plan and according to 1 Timothy 3:16, it describes it as "great is the mystery of godliness." The word mystery comes from the Greek word "musterion" which means a hidden plan, however, this same word is mentioned in 1 Corinthians 2:10 stating, "we speak the wisdom of God in a mystery, even the hidden wisdom, which God ordained before the world (KJV)" then it is appropriate to also look at the Hebrew word as well since the plan of GOD preceded the Greek term. The Hebrew equivalent to "musterion" is the term *"Sod" which means "secret (sod 05475) primarily means confidential conversation, speech or talk. Compare the Arabic word "sa'wada" which means to speak secretly. Sod emphasizes confidentiality in contrast to more general advice or counsel. Sod can refer to the close friendship which exists between people (Psalms 55:14)* or to the intimate knowledge that friendship brings, especially their secrets (Proverbs 25:9). F B Meyer commenting on the use of sod in Ps 25:14-note rightly reminds us of "What secrets God has to tell His own!" (Genesis 18:17; John 14:21, 23, 15:15; 1 Corinthians 2:9, 10)." [1] In other words, GOD's musterion/sod is His hidden plan or secret that he only reveals to His friends in confidence.

This is to say that God's foreknowledge is his hidden plan that he kept secret before the world began. All those who believed in Him joined in this predestined plan and were elected into the plan that God foreknew He was going to bring into fruition at an appointed time. Let us just look at this great predestined plan GOD had through the scriptures.

*Acts 2:23 Him, being delivered by the determinate counsel and **foreknowledge** of God, ye have taken, and by wicked hands have crucified and slain: (KJV).*

*Matthew 13:35 That it might be fulfilled which was spoken by the prophet, saying, I will open my mouth in parables; **I will utter things which have been kept secret from the foundation of the world**. (KJV)*

*Revelation 13:8 And all that dwell upon the earth shall worship him, whose names are not written in the book of life of **the Lamb slain from the foundation of the world** (KJV).*

*Hebrews 9:26 For then must he often have **suffered since the foundation of the world**: but now once in the end of the world hath he* *appeared to put away sin by the sacrifice of himself. (Heb 9:26 KJV)*

*Hebrews 4:3 For we which have believed do enter into rest, as he said, As I have sworn in my wrath, if they shall enter into my rest: although **the works were finished from the foundation of the world**. (KJV)*

*1 Peter 1:2 **Elect** according to the **foreknowledge** of God the Father, through sanctification of the Spirit, unto obedience and sprinkling of the blood of Jesus Christ: Grace unto you, and peace, be multiplied (KJV).*

*1 Peter 1: 18-20 Forasmuch as ye know that ye were not redeemed with corruptible things, as silver and gold, from your vain conversation received by tradition from your fathers; 19 But with the precious blood of Christ, as of a lamb without blemish and without spot: 20 Who verily was **foreordained before the foundation of the world**, but was manifest in these last times for you (KJV).*

*1 Corinthians 2:7,10 But **we speak the wisdom of God in a mystery**, even the **hidden wisdom**, which God **ordained before the world** unto our glory:But God hath revealed them unto us by his Spirit: for the Spirit searcheth all things, yea, the deep things of God. (KJV)*

Election, predestination, and foreknowledge are like a professional athletic franchise. Before the NFL, NBA, MLB, and other professional sporting leagues had players, they drew up a business plan to start a league, and then they began to organize teams along with where the headquarters, cities, and states would be located. Once their plans were complete, then, they began to look for players, and they did it through a draft. The owners had already created a team without the players, but players had to be selected to be on the team. The team is like the plan of GOD, and when GOD created the plan to form the Body of Christ, GOD did it before the foundation of the world, which solidified GOD's plan. Whoever is chosen by their free will to be a part of this great assembly that GOD foreknew because He predestined it can join as the elect or, in other words, chosen of GOD. We are all elected to a plan that GOD foreknew. I work for a company as an administrator, and I have to discuss the history of the institution at times, even though I was not a part of its inception, I always speak of it in terms of how our company has experienced success for over one hundred years because I am now a part of that history. This is the idea of GOD's foreknowledge, predestination, and election. The problem is when the Bible speaks about foreknowledge, predestination, and election, it uses plural pronouns but as readers, we see individual selves in that plural and we read it as if he knew us ahead of time and elected and predestined us individually ahead of time and before the world and that is not the correct interpretation. Just as in Ephesians 1:4, where the plural pronoun "us" is illuding to the Body of Christ and not an individual. "According as he hath chosen us in him before the foundation of the world, that we should be holy and without blame before him in love (Eph 1:4 KJV)."

Let me take it a step further, going back to the professional athletic teams. Some players do not follow the teams' rules and can get released. This is the same for the Body of Christ. In 1 Timothy 4:1, it says, Now the Spirit speaketh expressly, that in the latter times, some shall depart from the faith, giving heed to seducing spirits, and doctrines of devils (KJV)." There will be a time of apostasy in the last days, and many will desert the faith. This is in contradiction to eternal security. GOD states in Deuteronomy 30:19 "I call heaven and earth to record this day against you, that I have set before you life and death, blessing and cursing: therefore choose life, that both thou and thy seed may live (KJV)." This is GOD saying you have the choice to choose which route you take, and in Joshua 24:15, Joshua makes a commitment that he and his household choose to serve GOD.

If predestination, foreknowledge, and election are for select people, then why Matthew 22:14 states, "For many are called, but few are chosen (KJV)." This aligns with John 3:16 that GOD loves the entire world, but it is whoever believes that receives eternal salvation. The doctrine of eternal security is one of the slipperiest slopes to teach believers because if they believe they are eternally secure then they have no conviction to live a holy and sanctified life. The majority of the New Testament admonishes believers how to live a life set apart from the world and be different. Hebrews 12:14 states, Follow peace with all men, and holiness, without which no man shall see the Lord (KJV)." If we are eternally secure then why do we have to endure to the end to be saved as mentioned in Matt 24:13. Salvation must require us to abstain from worldly lust (1 Pet 2:11) and the only way we can reign with JESUS is if we endure and suffer with him as stated in 2 Timothy 2:12.

The book of Hebrews 10:26 state, "For if we sin willfully after that we have received the knowledge of the truth, there remaineth no more sacrifice for sins (KJV). Furthermore, the book of Hebrews 6:4-6 states, "For it is impossible for those who were once enlightened, and have tasted of the heavenly gift, and were made partakers of the Holy Ghost, 5 And have tasted the good word of God, and the powers of the world to come, 6 If they shall fall away, to renew them again unto repentance; seeing they crucify to themselves the Son of God afresh, and put him to an open shame (KJV)." Finally, if eternal security is true, then why does the dissertation of Paul in the book of Romans chapter eleven discuss how some of the branches were broken off, speaking of Israel, and how some branches were grafted in, speaking of the Gentiles? In Romans 11:21 clearly says, "F or if God spared not the natural branches, take heed lest he also spare not thee (KJV)."

CHAPTER 17 TRINITY DOCTRINE

Miseducation: The father, son, and the Holy Spirit are the three persons in the godhead.

1 John 5:7

---

1 John 5:7 For there are three that bear record in heaven, the Father, the Word, and the Holy Ghost: and these three are one. (KJV)

The subject of this chapter is not meant to attack Christianity, God, or Christian believers despite the indoctrination that has developed since the start of the church. This is a chapter to seek out the truth by getting a biblical view of the nature of God. By doing this I must give attention to the most dominating theology in Christianity, which is the Trinity. Even though the Trinity is the most dominating theology when it comes to describing the nature of God, it is also the most problematic theology in the history of the Christian Church. There have been many controversies, debates, and even violence over the centuries because of this theology. This is an attempt to explain the nature of GOD through Bible scriptures and not adhere to theology that is outside the teachings of the Bible, but rather present a Biblical view versus the Trinity or the Triune view of GOD. In order to do that I must present the problems that the Trinity presents when it comes to explaining the nature of God. A Biblical view of the nature of GOD will not create another theology or view of the nature of God but try to present a true orthodox view of the nature of God.

It was Tertullian (c.160-230) who first coined the term *trinitas* from which the English word 'trinity' comes from. He clarifies thus the "mystery of the divine economy... which of the unity makes a trinity, placing the three in order not of quality but of sequence, different not in substance but in aspect, not in power but in manifestation."[1] At other times he used other images to show his point, such as the monarchy: "... If he who is the monarch has a son, and if the son is given a share in the monarchy, this does not mean that the monarchy is automatically divided, ceasing to be a monarchy."[2] Again, Tertullian explains the concept of being brought forth: "As the root brings forth the shoot, as the spring brings forth the stream, as the sun brings forth the beam."[3] Tertullian did not consider the Father and Son co-eternal: "There was a time when there was neither sin to make God a judge, nor a son to make God a Father;"[4] nor did he consider them co-equal: "For the Father is the whole substance, whereas the Son is something derived from it."[5] In Tertullian we find a groundwork upon which a trinity concept can be founded, but it has not yet evolved into that trinity of the Nicene Creed. The Trinitarian doctrine was established at the council of Nicea. It was more than one hundred years after the crucifixion of Christ that Tertullian coined the word 'trinity.' The key words from the Nicene debate, like *homoousis* and *ousis* are not Biblical but were an attempt to silence the Arian controversy.

The three most famous Christian creeds are the Apostles, Nicene, and Athanasian (or Trinitarian). The words of these creeds show us a lot about the evolution of Trinitarian theology. These creeds were what birthed the three-in-one/one-in-three mystery of Father, Son, and Holy Ghost, making tritheism official. This creed has many complications, and not just how it is worded but also how it was enforced and why it was enforced is important.

Godhead

In explaining the Trinity, people will often use the phrase that there are "three persons in the Godhead." This is another problem in scripture, and I would go as far as to say that it is reverse theology. It is reverse theology because the scriptures never teach that there are three persons in the Godhead or any number at all. The scripture teaches in Colossians 2:9 states:

> "[that] the fullness of the Godhead bodily dwells in him (KJV)."

The word Godhead in the Bible comes from the Greek word "Theotētos Θεότητος," which the King James Version translated as Godhead, but the word is deity, and the scripture in Colossians 2:9 teaches that fullness of God is dwelling in Jesus. The NET translation brings more clarity as it says:

> For in him all the fullness of deity lives[a] in bodily form, (Col 2:9 NET)

This text does not teach that there are three persons in the Godhead but contrasts that the Godhead is in JESUS. "The present tense in this verse ("lives") is significant. As was said in Colossians 1:19, all of GOD's fullness dwells in JESUS; this is not a temporary dwelling, but a permanent one. Paul's point is polemical against the idea that the fullness of God dwells anywhere else, as the Gnostics believed, except in Christ alone."[6] I heard a question once that said, "Is God one who and three what's, or is GOD one what and three who's? In a sarcastic way but very profound was the answer, saying, "GOD is one who and can be as many what's as he wants to be." Have we lost sight that GOD is GOD and what makes him God is he can do things unimaginable to the human intellect. The Trinity is a search to explain GOD in the realm of understanding him through human intelligence instead of using the spiritual truths of the Bible.

In hearing the explanation of the Trinity from many theologians sounds very arbitrary. The authority of their view of GODs nature does not have a strong scripture base. When most trinitarian theologians are questioned by people that try to get a better understanding about the doctrine of the Trinity they hide under the umbrella of it being a mystery. In this case any theologian of a heterodoxic doctrine of the nature of GOD could do the same thing and claim mystery to their doctrine. But what usually happens is they are called a heretic and is accused of erroneous teachings. The word mystery is not an excuse. They word mystery in the Bible comes from the Greek word "musterion [which means] a secret, or "mystery" (through the idea of silence imposed by initiation into religious rites)."[7] The definition states that, yes, it is a secret, but the according to the scriptures in I Corinthians 2:10, that secret is supposed to be revealed to all Spirit-filled believers. In verse seven of chapter 2 in Corinthians, it begins to say how "we speak the wisdom of God in a mystery, even the hidden wisdom, which God ordained before the world to our glory (KJV)." When scripture mentions this mystery, it not only states that we speak it but in verse ten, it says, "God hath revealed them unto us by his Spirit for the Spirit searches all things, yea, the deep things of God (KJV)." So, the nature of God is not a mystery when we cannot explain it. We choose to hide behind the word mystery when we have constructed a theology that has flaws in it. I Timothy 3:15 states, Great is the mystery of godliness: God was manifest in the flesh (KJV)." This is a mystery that was revealed to Paul that Jesus was not the second person in the Godhead but it was God revealed in the flesh but instead of using the Biblical view of scriptures, the Trinitarian view has caused many to look at the scriptures through the lens of the Trinity and visions the second person of the Godhead instead of envisioning the simple fact that it was just God that was incarnate. Harry Rimmer speaks of the mystery in his book titled "The Purposes of Calvary." Rimmer speaks of the original meaning of the ancient word. He says, "The word was a military term that had been coined by the Ptolemies. These great rulers had a company of relatives called "Philos," who constituted their cabinet and board of strategy. When they planned warfare, the "Philos" met and prepared a plan of battle or, rather, a stratagem for the campaign.[8] This plan was kept so secret that even the officers of the army were in ignorance of its details and objectives. Thus, the enemies were unable to plan the defeat of the strategy and campaign. This military plan was called the "musterion" – and the enemy was unable to discover its purpose until the plan unfolded to his undoing, if all went well."[9] The mystery was a secret "which none of the princes of the world knew it, for had they known, they would not have crucified the Lord of Glory (I Cor. 2:8, KJV), but now the mystery is revealed. It is ludicrous for a believer to say that the nature of God is a mystery because the nature of God is supposed to be made known now according to scriptures. The plan was only a secret from the enemy, so if believers hide under that umbrella called the mystery, it makes me wonder if they truly know God. Not only that but the Hebrew equivalent of musterion is "sod" which is a secret revealed among friends and if a person claims they cannot fully understand who GOD is then they are not a friend of GOD and is lost because "if our gospel be hid, it is hid to them that are lost (2 Corinthians 4:3, KJV)."

Origin of Trinity in Pagan Religions

While the majority of the Christian world considers the concept of the Trinity vital to Christianity, many historians and Bible scholars agree that the Trinity of Christianity owes more to Greek philosophy and pagan polytheism than to the monotheism of the Jew and the Jewish Jesus. The search for the origins of the Trinity begins with the earliest writings of man. Records of early Mesopotamian and Mediterranean civilizations show polytheistic religions, though many scholars assert that the earliest man believed in one god. The 19th-century scholar and Protestant minister Alexander Hislop devoted several chapters of his book, "The Two Babylons," showing how this original belief in one god was replaced by the triads of paganism, which were eventually absorbed into Catholic Church dogmas. The historian S. H. Hooke tells in detail of the ancient Sumerian trinity: Anu was the primary god of heaven, the 'Father', and the 'King of the Gods'; Enlil, the "wind-god" was the god of the earth, and a creator god; and Enki was the god of waters and the 'lord of wisdom'."[10] The historian, H. W. F. Saggs, explains that the Babylonian triad consisted of 'three gods of roughly equal rank... whose inter-relationship is of the essence of their natures.'"[11] Hislop furthers the comparison, "In the unity of that one, Only God of the Babylonians there were three persons, and to symbolize [sic] that doctrine of the Trinity, they employed... the equilateral triangle, just as it is well known the Roman Church does at this day.'"[12]

Egypt's history is similar to Sumeria in antiquity. In his Egyptian Myths, George Hart, lecturer for the British Museum and professor of ancient Egyptian hieroglyphics at the University of London, shows how Egypt also believed in a "transcendental, above creation, and preexisting' one, the god Amun. Amun was really three gods in one. Ra was his face, Ptah his body, and Amun his hidden identity."[13] The well-known historian Will Durant concurs that Ra, Amon, and Ptah were "combined as three embodiments or aspects of one supreme and triune deity."[14] Additionally, a hymn to Amun written in the 14th century BC defines the Egyptian trinity as "All Gods are three: Amun, Re, Ptah; they have no equal. His name is hidden as Amun, he is Re... before [men], and his body is Ptah."[15] Durant submits that "from Egypt came the ideas of a divine trinity."[16] Dr. Gordon Laing, agrees that "the worship of the Egyptian triad Isis, Serapis, and the child Horus" probably accustomed the early church theologians to the idea of a triune God, and was influential "in the formulation of the doctrine of the Trinity as set forth in the Nicaean and Athanasian creeds."[17] These were not the only trinities early Christians were exposed to. The historical lecturer, Jesse Benedict Carter, tells us of the Etruscans. As they slowly passed from Babylon through Greece and went on to Rome,[18] they brought with them their trinity of Tinia, Uni, and Menerva. This trinity was a "new idea to the Romans," and yet it became so "typical of Rome" that it quickly spread throughout Italy.[19] Even the names of the Roman trinity: Jupiter, Juno, and Minerva, reflect the ancestry. Christianity was not ashamed to borrow from pagan culture according to Durant: "Christianity did not destroy paganism; it adopted it."[20] Laing convincingly devotes his entire book, "Survival of the Roman Gods," to the comparison of Roman paganism and the Roman Catholic Church. Dr. Jaroslav Pelikan, a Catholic scholar, confirms the Church's respect for pagan ideas when he says that the Apologists and other early church fathers used and cited the [pagan] Roman Sibylline Oracles so much that they were called "Sibyllists" by the 2nd-century critic, Celsus. The attitude of the Church toward paganism is summed up in Pope Gregory the Great's words to a missionary: "You must not interfere with any traditional belief or religious observance that can be harmonized with Christianity."[21]

After the captivity of the children of Israel, the Israelites came out of Babylonian captivity with paganistic views and split into two fractions. The Bible described them as Pharisees and Sadducees, but they were also known as Hellenists and Anti-Hellenists. One group was adhering to the law and the other became paganistic in their beliefs. This is also how the language Aramaic evolved because it was a mixed language between Hebrew and the Babylonian language of Akkadian. Below you will see the images of the Trinity preadoption of the Christian Trinity:

Babylonia

"The ancient Babylonians recognized the doctrine of a trinity, or three persons in one god—as appears from a composite god with three heads forming part of their mythology, and the use of the equilateral triangle, also, as an emblem of such trinity in unity."[22]

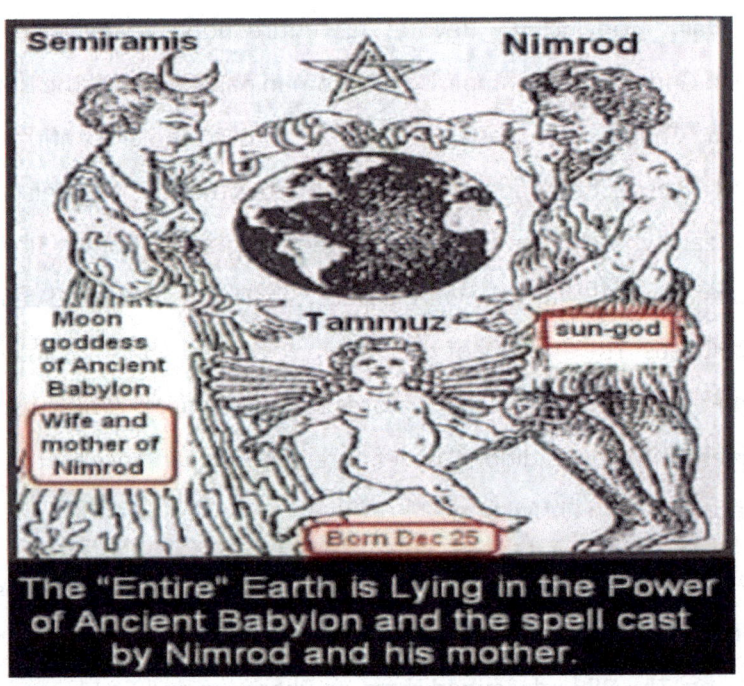

Egypt

"The Hymn to Amun decreed that 'No god came into being before him (Amun)' and that 'All gods are three: Amun, Re, and Ptah, and there is no second to them. Hidden is his name as Amon, he is Re in face, and his body is Ptah.' . . . This is a statement of trinity, the three chief gods of Egypt subsumed into one of them, Amon. The concept of organic unity within plurality got an extraordinary boost with this formulation. Theologically, in a crude form, it came strikingly close to the later Christian form of plural Trinitarian monotheism."[23]

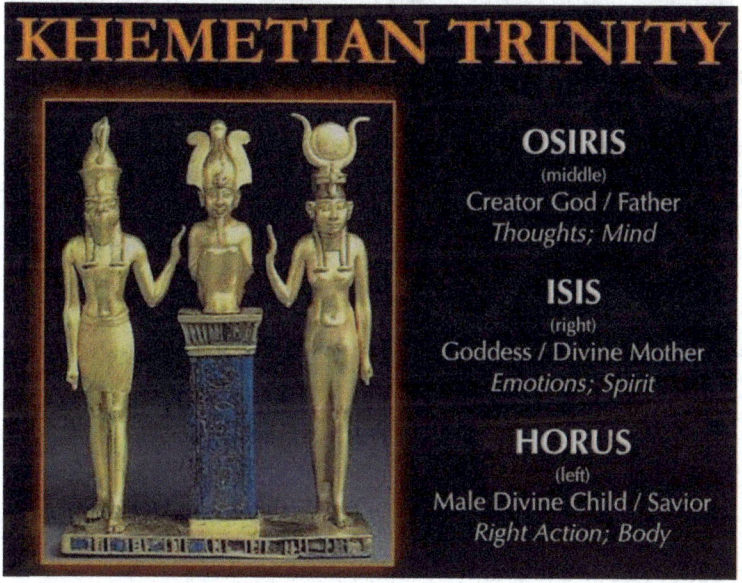

Sumeria

"The universe was divided into three regions each of which became the domain of a god. Anu's share was the sky. The earth was given to Enlil. Ea became the ruler of the waters. Together they formed the triad of the Great Gods."[24]

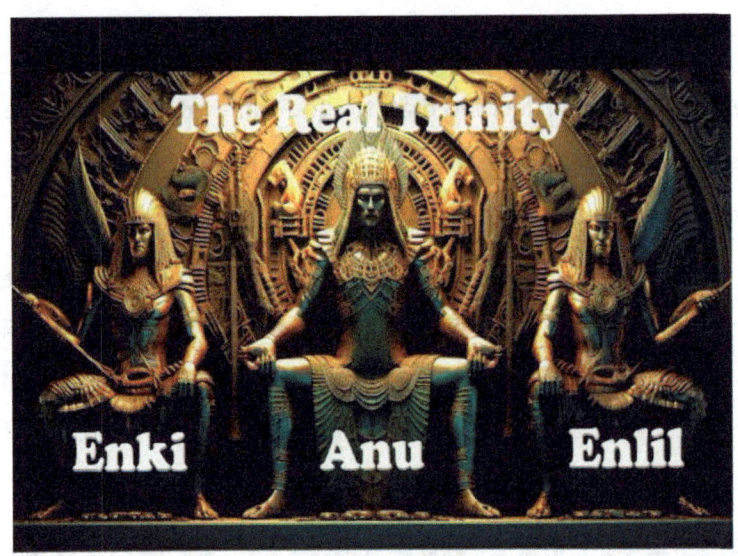

India

"The Puranas, one of the Hindoo Bibles of more than 3,000 years ago, contain the following passage: 'O ye three Lords! know that I recognize only one God. Inform me, therefore, which of you is the true divinity, that I may address to him alone my adorations.' The three gods, Brahma, Vishnu, and Siva [or Shiva], becoming manifest to him, replied, 'Learn, O devotee, that there is no real distinction between us. What to you appears such is only the semblance. The single being appears under three forms by the acts of creation, preservation, and destruction, but he is one.'

"Hence the triangle was adopted by all the ancient nations as a symbol of the Deity . . . Three was considered among all the pagan nations as the chief of the mystical numbers, because, as Aristotle remarks, it contains within itself a beginning, a middle, and an end. Hence, we find it designating some of the attributes of almost all the pagan gods."[25]

Greece

"In the Fourth Century B.C. Aristotle wrote: 'All things are three, and thrice is all: and let us use this number in the worship of the gods; for, as the Pythagoreans say, everything and all things are bounded by threes, for the end, the middle and the beginning have this number in everything, and these compose the number of the Trinity.'"[26]

Other areas

Many other areas had their own divine trinities. In Greece, they were Zeus, Poseidon, and Adonis. The Phoenicians worshipped Ulomus, Ulosuros and Eliun. Rome worshipped Jupiter, Neptune, and Pluto. In Germanic nations they were called Wodan, Thor and Fricco. Regarding the Celts, one source states, "The ancient heathen deities of the pagan Irish[,] Criosan, Biosena, and Seeva, or Sheeva, are doubtless the Creeshna [Krishna], Veeshnu [Vishnu], [or the all-inclusive] Brahma, and Seeva [Shiva], of the Hindoos."[27]

Nowhere in the Bible is the Trinity mentioned. If the Trinity did not originate with the Bible, where did it come from? To find the origins of the Trinity in Christianity, we need to take a look at the circumstances in which early Christians found themselves. Even the Church of the Apostles' day was far from unified. The Apostle Paul wrote to the Thessalonians that 'the mystery of iniquity doth already work (2Th 2:7, KJV)." Gnosticism was an early influence on Christians. Gnosticism was predominant in this ancient period, it behooves one to learn what they believed, for many early church writings were defenses against Gnosticism. Gnosticism borrowed much of its philosophy and religion from Mithraism, oriental mysticism, astrology, magic, and Plato. It considered matter to be evil and in opposition to Deity, relied heavily on visions, and sought salvation through knowledge. Arthur Cushman McGiffert interprets some of the early Christian fathers as believing the Gnosticism to be 'identical to all intents and purposes with Greek polytheism."[28] Gnosticism had a mixed influence on the early Christian writers. Not only was the Church divided by Gnosticism, enticed by philosophy, and set upon by paganism, but there was a geographic division as well. The East (centered in Alexandria) and the West (centered in Rome) grew along two different lines. The East was intellectually adventurous and speculative, reflecting the surrounding Greek culture. Clement and Origen represent the theological development of the East.

Clement of Alexandria (c. 150-220) was from the "Catechetical School" of Alexandria. His views were influenced by Gnosticism,[29] and McGiffert affirms, "Clement insists that philosophy came from God and was given to the Greeks as a schoolmaster to bring them to Christ as the law was a schoolmaster for the Hebrews."[30] McGiffert further states that Clement considered "God the Father revealed in the Old Testament" separate and distinct from the "Son of God incarnate in Christ," with whom he identified the Logos."[31] It is the "Logos doctrine" that created what we know today as the eternal Son of God theory. This is another theology forced into Christianity to support the Trinity. Jesus's sonship was predetermined in God's mind and plan for eternity, but he did not exist until he was born in Bethlehem. When a homebuilder looks at blueprints of his future home, they see the plans for the bathroom and say, "There's the bathroom." They can see it in their mind's eye, but it does not exist yet. The plan of Jesus' birth, life, sacrifice, and death was similar. You might say, God had a blueprint of salvation that was so real to him he could see it as though it already existed. Romans 4:17 tells us "God...calls things that are not as though they were." Psalm 2:7 (quoted above) in the KJV states "this day have I begotten thee." Jesus was God's son, his only son—he had a birthday which means there was a time when he did not exist. The spirit of God is eternal, without beginning or end. Man is not eternal. As a man, Jesus had a beginning. The humanity of Jesus died as a sacrifice for our sins at Calvary. The spirit of the risen Christ, humanity and divinity together will never end. Since the first Christmas day, Jesus will always be God, and God will always be man. 1 Corinthians 15:28 describes a time when "God will be all, and in all." The sonship of Jesus as mediator to the human race will no longer be necessary when there is no more sin, no more death, no more sorrow. Jesus will always be God's only begotten son. John 1 supports the eternal Son of God:1, 2, which states, "In the beginning was the Word, and the Word was with God, and the Word was God. The same was in the beginning with God (KJV)." In looking at this scripture we must think of how John was thinking. He could not have been thinking of the logos in the Greek was of thinking of it. But he was an Aramaic speaking man and even though we have the word logos from the Greek, John was thinking with his Jewish mind. The word that would replace logos in Aramaic would be

"Memra." This means a thought or concept. That means the Son of God was only a thought or concept in GOD's plan.

The person who is considered to be the founder of theology is Origen (c.185-253), who is considered by,[32] some to be "the greatest scholar of the early church and the greatest theologian of the East (p. 38)."[33] Durant adds that "with [Origen] Christianity ceased to be only a comforting faith; it became a full-fledged philosophy, buttressed with scripture but proudly resting on reason."[34] According to Pelikan's Historical Theology, Origen was the "teacher of such orthodox stalwarts as the Cappadocian Fathers" but also the "teacher of Arius" and the "originator of many heresies."[35] Centuries after his death, he was condemned by councils at least five times; however, both Athanasius and Eusebius had great respect for him.

As he tried to reckon the 'incomprehensible God' with both Stoic and Platonic philosophy, Origen presented views that could support both sides of the Trinity argument. He believed the Father and Son were separate "in respect of hypostasis" (substance), but "one by harmony and concord and identity of will."[36] He claimed the Son was the image of God which has strong Biblical claims. Jesus is the "exact representation of his being" according to Hebrew 1:3 (NIV), He "is the image of God" according to II Corinthians 4:4 (KJV), and "He is the image of the invisible God" according to Colossians 1:15 (KJV). According to John 4:24, "God is spirit." Luke 24:39 tells us "a spirit has no flesh or bone." All scripture confirms that God, in the Old Testament, was invisible. "No man has seen God" (John 1:18, KJV); but

Jesus' description is the "exact representation of God, the image of God, and the image of the invisible God." The spirit of God never permanently occupied a body or form before, took on the form of a man by becoming the person of Jesus Christ. He was no longer invisible, untouchable, without form; now, he dwelt among us. Both God Almighty and man were born in Bethlehem as Jesus Christ.

The world around the early Church was changing. The Roman Empire began to crumble, and Constantine came to power. He wished to unify the Empire and chose Christianity to do so. But Christianity was far from unified. It is an oversight in history that the emperor who presided over the council was a pagan worshiper. Even though Constantine made Christianity legal he was still a Sun Worshiper. The council was not a fair council and was hardly Spirit-led as made to believe. This council used Mafia-type tactics. Constantine was brought into the decision-making process because he had the authority to decide by emperor status and the decision would have to be obeyed by his kingdom. Whichever way Constantine would be swayed, that is who won the debate. Nicean bishops persuaded Constantine to condemn Arius, his followers, and his doctrine. It was 325 A.D. at Nicaea that Athanasius and Eusebius presented the doctrine of the Trinity since Arius was not a bishop and only bishops could attend. The council hoped to explain through scripture, but using scripture would have given Arianism some support in its doctrine, so it produced the Trinitarian Creed. Constantine was never indeed swayed. Constantine invited Arius to a conference six years later by persuasion of Eusebius, who was known to be a distant relative. Constantine removed the expulsion of Athanasius and Arius restoring their bishoprics. Constantine adopted the Arian view and then exiled the Nicean bishops. Eusebius of Nicomedia, baptize him; and had his son and successor, Constantius, raised as an Arian. So there goes the belief that the council was Spirit-led. The decision of who would be in power at the Nicean councils was based on who could persuade Constantine. Constantine himself thought of himself as God-incarnate and did not try to make a full conversion to Christianity until he was on his deathbed and was baptized by the believers of Arianism. The controversy of the Trinity doctrine has been debated for decades and centuries by those who oppose it and its proponents. The Nicea council strongly needed more unity of thought among the proponents that supported the Trinity doctrine. Lonergan goes on to explain that the language of debate on the consubstantiality of the Father and the Son has made many people think that the "Church at Nicea had abandoned the genuine Christian doctrine, which was religious through and through, in order to embrace some sort of Hellenistic ontology (p. 128)"[37] which is not farfetched because before the church came into existence there were major Hellenistic influences across the Roman Empire that even caused schisms within the Jewish community. He concludes that the Nicene dogma marked the "transition from the prophetic Oracle of Yahweh... to Catholic dogma."[38]

There is much proof that the Trinity owes it origins to paganism and philosophy. The evidence of history leaves little doubt. The concept of the Trinity finds its roots in Pagan theology and Greek philosophy. Historically, this "doctrine of God" has proved to be a bloody doctrine that has no relation to the true God of love, or His Son Jesus Christ. Durant details the problems that arose from the Council at Nicea and summarizes that period with a dreadful verdict: "Probably more Christians were slaughtered by Christians in these two years than by all the persecutions of Christians by pagans in the history of Rome."[39] Thus they perverted the teachings of Christ: "Love thy neighbor as thyself," (Mt 19:19) and of his apostles: "If we love one another, God dwelleth in us, and His love is perfected in us (1Jo 4:12)." Elements and the evolution of the Trinity could be seen in the words of the Apostles' Creed, Nicene Creed, and the Athanasian Creed. As each of the creeds became wordier and convoluted, the simple, pure faith of the Apostolic church became lost in a haze. Even more interesting is the fact that as the creeds became more specific (and less scriptural) the adherence to them became stricter, and the penalty for disbelief harsher.

The Old Testament is filled with scriptures such as "before Me there was no God formed, neither shall any be after Me" (Isa. 43:10), and "there is no other God...I am the Lord, and there is none else" (Isa. 45:14, 18). A Jewish commentary affirms that "[no] other gods exist, for to declare this would be blasphemous... (Chumash 458)."[40] Even though "Word," "Spirit," "Presence," and "Wisdom" are used as personifications of God, Biblical scholars agree that the Trinity is neither mentioned nor intended by the authors of the Old Testament.[41] There are a few scriptures that are used to support the Trinitarian view compared to thousands of other scriptures that do not support that view. In Biblical interpretation, there can be no single text of the Bible that can contradict the general truth of the Bible. The general truth is that God is one, alone in creation; there is no other deity besides Him. There are over 10,000 Bible texts that either implicitly or explicitly declare the absolute, solitary Oneness of God. Implicit texts declare that God is a solitary one using singular pronouns, verbs, and adjectives when referring to God Almighty. An example of this is Gen. 1:27: "So God created man in his own image, in the image of God created he him (KJV)" As well as 1 Kings 11:33 and Ezekiel 13:8. Explicit texts clearly say that God is One and alone in His reign. An example of this is Deuteronomy 6:4, the Hebrew Shema, which states, "Hear, O Israel: The LORD our God is one LORD (cf. Mark 12:29) (KJV)." Other examples are Job 9:8, Isaiah 44:6, Isaiah 44:24, Malachi 2:10, Mark 12:28-31, 1 Timothy 2:5, and James 2:19.

In the interpretation of the scriptures, there are verses that are difficult to understand and must be interpreted considering verses that are more easily understood. Less than ten verses in the Bible are misunderstood because they are not properly interpreted. Examples: **Genesis. 1:26** "Let us make man in our image (KJV)," **Genesis 3:22** "And the LORD God said, Behold, the man is become as one of us, to know good and evil: and now, lest he put forth his hand, and take also of the tree of life, and eat, and live forever (KJV)," **Genesis 11:7** "Go to, let us go down, and there confound their language, that they may not understand one another's speech (KJV)" **Isaiah 6:8** "Also I heard the voice of the Lord, saying, Whom shall I send, and who will go for us? Then said I, Here am I; send me (KJV)," **Matthew 28:19** "Go ye therefore, and teach all nations, baptizing them in the name of the

Father, and of the Son, and of the Holy Ghost (KJV)," II Corinthians 13:14 "The grace of the Lord Jesus Christ, and the love God, and the communion of the Holy Ghost, be with you all. Amen (KJV)," and **1 John 5:7** "For there are three that bear record in heaven, the Father, the Word, and the Holy Ghost: and these three are one (KJV)." However, there is no Greek text that supports this translation. The Greek text for 1 John 5:7 is rendered "ὅτι τρεῖς εἰσιν οἱ μαρτυροῦντες, (SBLT)." These five Greek words could not be translated as the English version, but in the NET translation, it is correct as it is translated as "For there are three that testify."

The verses above can be difficult to understand if approached without a firm understanding of God's personality presented in the rest of the Bible. Jesus is God Almighty according to Isaiah 9:6, Isaiah 7:14, and Matthew 1:23. The declaration of Jesus as the Mighty God and Everlasting Father was long before his conception in the womb of Mary. The Everlasting Father became the child and son born in the manger. Therefore, Jesus truly is Immanuel, God with us. Jesus is Almighty. God becomes a man according to Isaiah 40:3 and John 1:23. In prophecy, John the Baptist was to prepare the world to receive God Almighty. John prepared the world for Jesus, preaching the message of repentance. John did not make a mistake; he knew that Jesus was Jehovah God joining humanity. Isaiah 45:23 quotes God to say, "Every knee will bow...every tongue will swear." In the previous verses, God said: "...there is no God apart from me, a righteous God and a Savior; there is none but me...there is no other." In Philippians, Paul, a Pharisee, uses this same language to refer to Jesus. He understood scripture's description of God as a solitary spirit, a lone sovereign. He also knew that applying this scripture to Jesus was the same as calling him the only true God. In essence, Paul was saying that Jesus was the only God and God is Savior, become a man according to Isaiah 44:6, Isaiah 48:12, and Revelation 22:13. God declared through Isaiah that he was the "first and the last," but Jesus went further with his declaration by claiming to be the "Alpha and Omega, first and last, beginning and end." How many "firsts and lasts" are there? The only correct explanation is found in the fact that Jesus is Almighty God incarnate.

Jesus' Father, the Spirit of God, was living within him according to John 10:30, 38, John 14:8-10, 20, 2 Corinthians 5:19, and Colossians 1:19. Have you ever asked yourself the question: *When Jesus prayed, to whom was he praying? Why did Jesus have such a subordinate role if he was God Almighty?* Jesus was born a male child of the human race. He needed food, water, warmth, and nurturing to survive and flourish. Jesus became tired; he slept; he wept. He was tempted in every aspect possible. The humanity of Jesus was as fragile and susceptible to failure as any other human being. The difference between Jesus and us, is Jesus had total access to the Spirit of God living in him. John the Baptist described Jesus by saying: "For the one whom God has sent speaks the words of God, for God gives the Spirit without limit" (John 3:34, NIV). It was the Spirit of God living in Jesus that gave him the power to do miracles, to know the thoughts of men, and to be "God with us." The humanity of Jesus prayed to the Spirit of God in him for strength, insight, wisdom, knowledge, direction, and power. The Spirit in Jesus was no longer just a temporary manifestation of the deity on earth. God became a man and became what he was not and remained who he was. The humanity of Jesus was the mediator between God and men (1 Timothy 2:5). The flesh and blood were necessary for the "propitiation of our sins (Romans 3:25, 1 John 2:2, 1 John 4:10, KJV);" "for without the shedding of blood, there can be no forgiveness of sin (Hebrews 9:22, KJV)." The importance of Jesus being a man does not end there. Jesus is also our advocate, defending us when we stand before God in judgment when the accuser tries to steal us away from God (Romans 8:34, Hebrews 7:25, 1 John 2:1). The humanity of Jesus should encourage every downtrodden, brokenhearted, defeated individual because in Jesus, we have someone who understands what we are going through. Jesus will always be a man, but he will not always need to be a mediator, an atonement for sin, an intercessor. God will always reside in Jesus; therefore, Jesus will always be God.

Jesus is the Holy Ghost/Comforter according to Matthew 28:20, John 14:16-18, and Romans 8:9-11. One must exercise caution to remember that the Holy Spirit is God's Spirit, not a separate entity. The words "Holy Spirit" are "pneuma hagion" in the Greek. Translated it means "holy breath." It was the holy breath of God that hovered over the waters in creation (Genesis 1:2). That same holy breath of God overshadowed Mary, the mother of Jesus, and then lived in his son. The holy breath of God raised Jesus from the dead. The spirit of the risen Christ referred to in these verses is the same holy breath of God. Only now, the spirit has taken up permanent residence in a man. Jesus told his followers in John 14: "I will not leave you comfortless, I will come to you" (KJV). He identifies himself as the comforter, which is one and the same as the Holy Spirit. In Romans, Paul refers to the Spirit of God living in you, and in the next phrase emphasizes the importance of having the Spirit of Christ in you. The connection should be simple.

Well, in presenting the history of the Trinity and that of scriptures it is clear that there is not enough proof of scripture to call God a Trinity. It is not fair to delegate God to a numerical value. The scriptures indicate that there is one God, and the Trinitarian doctrine has indoctrinated the minds of the believers to become closet pagans without notice. The believer has been forced to believe it without understanding it. Is not part of God's purpose for reconciling us to him that we may know him. It is said to try and understand the Trinity is to lose your mind and to not believe it is to lose your soul. This is a scare tactic that is not true and is not found anywhere in scripture. Jesus said, "But as many as received him, to them gave he power to become the sons of God, *even* to them that believe in his name: (John 1:12, KJV)." Jesus also said, "He that believeth on me, believeth not on me, but on him that sent me. And he that seeth me seeth him that sent me (John 12:44, 45, KJV). So, the point is to believe in Jesus, not the Trinity. The alternative view of the Trinity is to come back to a sound scriptural view of God and call him not Trinity but call him Jesus.

CHAPTER 18 NEW BIRTH/SALVATION DEBATE

Miseducation: There are many ways to be saved or experience a new birth in Christ.
1. You're saved by faith
2. Sinners Prayer
3. Roman road to salvation
4. Death Bed Confession
5. Biblical mode of salvation

In this chapter, we will discuss the New Testament birth or what is considered soteriology, which is the study of salvation. Professing Christians are very fractured in what they define as salvation. The first century church never gave so many options of how to become born again as modern believers do today. We will look at the list of different doctrines that are presented by so many denominations today. The adherents to these many beliefs would criticize others for calling them fundamentalists and legalists who are trying to work to earn salvation. First, I agree that a person cannot be saved by work, but a person should work because they are saved. In looking at the terms fundamentalist and legalism, they have two different meanings. Legalism is understood as the belief that a person can only be saved by adhering to the law or a devotion to (following the law with strict principles. It is really based on the attempt to merge the Old Testament law with the New Covenant principles, just as Peter and the Jewish Christians were attempting to enforce the Old Testament laws onto the Gentiles. Fundamentalism is a following of a basic set of rules that deems it necessary for an individual to adhere to the principles of their faith. I have no problem with following fundamentals because if a person desires to be successful in anything they do, whether it is a job, athletics, mechanics, driving a vehicle, or anything else, then they must follow the fundamentals of that activity to be successful. The scripture declares, "Behold, to obey is better than sacrifice, and to hearken than the fat of rams (1 Sam 15:22, KJV)" and Luke 6:46 states, "And why call ye me, Lord, Lord, and do not the things which I say (KJV)?"

Are You Saved by Faith Alone?

The first doctrine to be discussed is the belief that we are saved by faith and faith alone. This belief is in opposition to being saved by works. You cannot Be saved by works, but you cannot be saved by faith only, either. There have been many proponents of the belief that people are saved by faith and faith alone. The first scripture that many believers in Christ subscribe to is that we are saved by faith. Ephesians 2:8 says, "For by grace are ye saved through faith; and that not of yourselves: it is the gift of God: (KJV)." This scripture does not say we are saved by faith, but on the contrary, it says, "we are saved by grace through faith." I will use an analogy that I heard Dr. Johnny James mention in discussing this text to describe the meaning. If a person is on top of a 10-story building that is on fire and the only choice is to jump the fire department brings a net to place at the bottom of the building in the direction of the person. If the person decides to jump, what saves the person, the jump or the net? Obviously, the net saved the man because if it were not a net there, the person would not be able to survive the impact of the ground. In this analogy, grace is the net, and faith is the jump. Leaving your former life is always a leap of faith; however, if you do not have the grace of GOD to catch you, then there is no saving.

To bring some clarity to the subject, works in the Bible have nothing to do with baptism, praying, fasting, or any other requirements that is instructed for believers to do. Works are described as things such as giving to the poor as clothing, food, helping, being kind, and being a good neighbor (Jam 2:15-16, Eph 4:32, Prov 19:17, Lk 6:27:38). The book of James chapter 2 put a noticeable clear stamp on the saved by faith alone subject:

---

14 What good is it, my brothers, if someone says he has faith but does not have works? Can that faith save him? 15 If a brother or sister has nothing to wear and has no food for the day, 16 and one of you says to them, "Go in peace, keep warm, and eat well," but you do not give them the necessities of the body, what good is it? 17 So also faith of itself, if it does not have works, is dead. 18 Indeed someone may say, "You have faith and I have works." Demonstrate your faith to me without works, and I will demonstrate my faith to you from my works. 19 You believe that God is one. You do well. Even the demons believe that and tremble. 20 Do you want proof, you ignoramus, that faith without works is useless? 21 Was not Abraham our father justified by works when he offered his son Isaac upon the altar? 22 You see that faith was active

> *along with his works, and faith was completed by the works. (James 2:14-22, NABRE)*

As the scripture clearly informs us that it is impossible to be saved by faith, but faith is clearly viewed by the works you do. The Bible does mention that we are justified by faith in Paul's writings in the Book of Romans 5:1, however, this is different from being saved by faith. Paul continues this same teachings to the church in Galatia where he mention, "Knowing that a man is not justified by the works of the law, but by the faith of Jesus Christ, even we have believed in Jesus Christ, that we might be justified by the faith of Christ, and not by the works of the law: for by the works of the law shall no flesh be justified (Gal 2:16, KJV), and Galatians 3:11, states, But that no man is justified by the law in the sight of God, it is evident: for, The just shall live by faith (KJV)." This is Paul's discourse on the difference between living by the law in contrast to living by faith. The law was a stumbling block for many of the believers that have come to the knowledge of the Messiah, and some were still trying to live by the law. James makes it clear "that a person is justified by works and not by faith alone (2:24, KJV)."

From a historical perspective, this teaching gained traction by Jacobus Faber (c. 1450-1536), who has been called "the father of the French reformation" (though he never formally left the Catholic Church), wrote a commentary on the epistles of Paul in 1512. This was five years before Luther's break with the Roman Church in Germany. In this volume, Faber argued that justification is obtained through faith without works."¹ Later, rebelling against the "merit works" system of Romanism, Luther would contend that salvation is based on "faith alone." According to one biographer, Luther exclaimed: "I, Doctor Martin Luther, unworthy herald of the gospel of our Lord Jesus Christ, confess this article, that faith alone without works justifies before God."² The doctrine of saved by faith alone was no more a rejection of the immoral eliciting of the Roman Catholic church and their way exploiting people for material gain through their preachers of indulgences which is no different than today preachers of prosperity.

Furthermore, JESUS gives a parable in the book of Matthew, chapter 25, verses 14-30, and gives talents to each servant based on their ability. To the servant that did much with the talent that was given was admonished and was told, "Well done, good and faithful servant; thou hast been faithful over a few things, I will make thee ruler over many things: enter thou into the joy of thy lord (21, KJV)." When the servant approached his lord and showed that he did nothing with the talent given him then, his lord was displeased, and "His lord answered and said unto him, Thou wicked and slothful servant, thou knewest that I reap where I sowed not, and gather where I have not strawed (26, KJV)." The end result of the slothful servant was outer darkness.

If GOD only requires faith to be saved, why is there so much emphasis on sanctification? GOD requires believers to be separate from the world and abstain from worldly lust as well as preserve to the end. Having faith means that because you trust and believe GOD then you will obey GOD's directions to get you to the destination of your eternal dwelling. Faith alone is an extrinsic way of believing because it requires no sacrifice and no effort, but JESUS mentions for all believers, "If any man will come after me, let him deny himself, and take up his cross daily, and follow me (Lk 9:23, KJV)."

There will be no lazy Christians in the Lamb's book life. Romans 12:11 states, "Not slothful in business; fervent in spirit; serving the Lord; (KJV)." This statement is not to refute having faith but just a reminder that we cannot sing standing on the promises while we sit on the premises! John 9:4 states, "We must perform the deeds of the one who sent me as long as it is daytime. Night is coming when no one can work (NET)." We show our faith, love, and dedication to our LORD, who paid it all by simply obeying Romans 12:1, "Therefore I exhort you, brothers and sisters, by the mercies of God, to present your bodies as a sacrifice– alive, holy, and pleasing to God– which is your reasonable service (Rom 12:1 NET)."

Sinners Prayer and Roman Road to Salvation

We will not discuss these doctrines in depth because they are discussed in chapter 9, titled "THE MISEDUCATION OF ROMANS 10:9 & THE SINNERS PRAYER." As mentioned in chapter nine, the sinner's prayer was developed as a rapid mass process to salvation. It is no more than a microwave formula to deal with the enormous crowds of the so-called crusade movements of the evangelicals. There is nowhere in scripture that shows that JESUS endorsed it or that the apostles used it as a formula for salvation. The notion of giving the preacher your hand, the secretary your name, and repeating words from the preacher does not qualify as a new birth experience. The most usual form of what is considered the sinner's prayer read as follows:

> *"Heavenly Father, I know that I am a sinner and that I deserve to go to heck. I believe that Jesus Christ died on the cross for my sins. I do now receive him as my Lord and personal Savior. I promise to serve you to the best of my ability. Please save me. In Jesus' name, Amen."*

This is the same as the phrases, accept the LORD, I gave myself to Christ, and even I found Christ. None of these phrases are possible, nor is it Biblical. In fact, we are in no position to accept a HOLY GOD; it is us who GOD accepts, according to Ephesians 1:6. The only thing we are able to do is to receive Him or receive the gracious opportunity to come into fellowship with the LORD, and He will give us the power to become the children of GOD according to John 1:12. The sinner's prayer eventually replaced the biblical role of water baptism. Though it is touted as gospel today, this prayer developed only recently. D. L. Moody was the first to employ it. Moody used this "model" of prayer when training his evangelistic coworkers.15 But it did not reach popular usage until the 1950s with Billy Graham's *Peace with God* tract and later with Campus Crusade for Christ's *Four Spiritual Laws.*"[3] To believe, therefore, that a sinner may be justified from sin by simply praying the sinner's prayer as a substitute for obedience to the plan of salvation, is to labor under a delusion that is void of biblical support. Undoubtedly, many who offer the sinner's prayer are exceedingly sincere. Sincerity alone, however, is unavailing (Prov. 14:12; Acts 23:1; 26:9).

Just as the "sinner's prayer" is not a Biblical doctrine for salvation, neither is what is considered the "Roman road to salvation." This doctrine came out of a misinterpretation from the book of Romans 10:9, which states, "That if thou shalt confess with thy mouth the Lord Jesus, and shalt believe in thine heart that God hath raised him from the dead, thou shalt be saved (KJV)." The key to understanding what Paul was talking about is found at the beginning of the chapter when he says, *"Brethren, my heart's desire and prayer to God for Israel is, that they might be saved. 2 For I bear them record that they have a zeal of God, but not according to knowledge. 3 For they being ignorant of God's righteousness, and going about to establish their own righteousness, have not submitted themselves unto the righteousness of God (Rom 10:1-3, KJV)."* Paul desired that the nation of Israel could experience the New Covenant's new birth experience, but because they were blinded according to Romans 11:25, he prayed to GOD that Israel would be saved. As the covenant people from the Old Testament, they did not believe JESUS was the Messiah and hoped that if they could only confess that JESUS was the LORD and believed that He was raised from the dead then they could be saved. There are two groups of Jews that Romans 10:9 addresses. The first is the Pharisees who did not believe JESUS was the messiah because the scripture in

Deuteronomy 21:23 states, "His body shall not remain all night upon the tree, but thou shalt in any wise bury him that day; (for he that is hanged is accursed of God;) that thy land be not defiled, which the Lord thy God giveth thee for an inheritance (KJV)." They could not understand that "Christ redeemed us from the curse of the law by becoming a curse for us, for it is written: "Cursed is everyone who is hung on a tree (Gal 3:14, KJV)." The Sadducees had a problem with the resurrection to the point where Paul was put on trial because of his beliefs. The Sadducees said, "For the Sadducees say that there is no resurrection, neither angel, nor spirit: but the Pharisees confess both. (Acts 23:8, KJV)." This is why Romans 10:9 appeals to both sets of Jews. Paul was a Jew himself and still had the heart to see his people saved, but he was commissioned as an apostle to the Gentiles (Rom 11:13). Another point to make is that the book of Romans was written to the church already established in Rome and this was not a book of instruction for salvation as the book of Acts. The outline of the book of Romans is as follows:

Romans' chapters 1-8: Righteousness and Justification

Romans' chapters 9-11: Jewish Program

Romans' chapters 12-16: Victorious Living in Christ Jesus

You cannot use chapters 9-11 to teach a doctrine of salvation for everyone when it is speaking to how GOD plans to deal with Israel.

Deathbed Confession

The death bed confession is another doctrine that has been used among believers as if a person could live as unrighteous as they feel liberty to do so, but when they feel their mortality slipping away someone can say a prayer and ask them if they accept the LORD into their life before they pass from this life. The scripture that adherents use to support this teaching is found in *Luke 23:39-43, stating "And one of the malefactors which were hanged railed on him, saying, If thou be Christ, save thyself and us. 40 But the other answering rebuked him, saying, Dost not thou fear God, seeing thou art in the same condemnation? 41 And we indeed justly; for we receive the due reward of our deeds: but this man hath done nothing amiss. 42 And he said unto Jesus, Lord, remember me when thou comest into thy kingdom. 43 And Jesus said unto him, Verily I say unto thee, Today shalt thou be with me in paradise (KJV)."* This scripture, like the others that were mentioned, was not taught by JESUS or his apostles as to how to be born again or receive salvation. When this act took place, it was before the New Testament church started, so technically, it happened under the Old Covenant. The church of the New Covenant was not started until the death, burial, and resurrection of the LORD, and the grand opening was on the Day of Pentecost when the Holy Spirit came as JESUS promised in John chapter fourteen. JESUS forgave sins all through His earthly ministry, but it was not for the doctrine of salvation for the New Covenant church. Since JESUS is GOD, then he can forgive whom he pleases and make allowances for "For he saith to Moses, I will have mercy on whom I will have mercy, and I will have compassion on whom I will have compassion (Rom 9:15, KJV)."

Biblical Mode of Salvation

When analyzing the Biblical mode of salvation or the new birth experience that was taught by the apostles of the LORD it is appropriate to use the book of Acts because the book of Acts is the history of the conception of the church. It is the book that introduces the church to the world after the crucifixion of JESUS the Messiah. It is the law of first mention that sets the precedent of how the church is to carry on what the LORD taught his disciples when he commissioned them to go out into the world and preach the gospel. Notice the chart below that breaks down every instance the apostles encountered people to describe what they must do to be saved.

New Testament Salvation

Who	Heard the gospel	Believed & Repented	Be baptized	Receive the Holy Spirit
Jews	Acts 2:37 when they heard this	Acts 2:38 Repent; Acts 2:41 received his word; Acts 2:44 all that believed	Acts 2:38 be baptized; Acts 2:41 were baptized	Acts 2:38 ye shall receive the gift of the Holy Spirit
Samaritans	Acts 8:5,6 Philip began proclaiming the Christ, as they heard	Acts 8:12 they believed Philip; Acts 8:14 Samaria had accepted the word	Acts 8:16 baptized in the name of the Lord Jesus	Acts 8:17 they received the Holy Spirit
Cornelius/ Gentiles	Acts 10:33 we are all here in the presence of God; Acts 10:44 those who heard the message	Acts 10:22 God-fearing man; Acts 10:43 everyone who believes in him receives forgiveness of sins through his name	Acts 10:48 have them baptized in the name of Jesus Christ	Acts 10:48 the gift of the Holy Spirit had been poured out even on the Gentiles, [46] for they heard them speaking in tongues
Apollos & followers (Believers)	Acts 19:5 When they heard this	Acts 18:24-28 Apollos was already a believer & preaching but was lacking understanding and Priscilla & Aquila explained to him more accurately the way of God	Acts 19:5 they were baptized in the name of the Lord Jesus	Acts 19:5 on them, the Holy Spirit came upon them, and they began to speak in tongues and to prophesy

JESUS' & the Apostle's Doctrine Concerning Salvation

The doctrine of Christ and His church (2 Jn. 1: 9) is the same today as it was during the first century, and no one has the right to amend it. Whosoever transgresseth, and abideth not in the doctrine of Christ, hath not God. He that abideth in the doctrine of Christ, he hath both the Father and the Son (2 John 1:9), KJV.)"

- We must be baptized to be saved (Mk. 16:16; Matt. 28:18-19).
- Baptism is for the remission of our sins (Acts 2:38).
- Our sins are washed away when we are baptized (Acts 22:16).
- We are saved when we are baptized (1 Pet. 3:21).
- The Lord adds us to the church when we are baptized (Acts 2:38-39, 40-41, 47).

Paul, the apostle of the LORD, saw errors creeping into the church even during his time of preaching. In his addressing the church of Galatia, he said, "6 I marvel that ye are so soon removed from him that called you into the grace of Christ unto another gospel: 7 Which is not another; but there be some that trouble you and would pervert the gospel of Christ. 8 But though we, or an angel from heaven, preach any other gospel unto you than that which we have preached unto you, let him be accursed. 9 As we said before, so say I now again, if any man preach any other gospel unto you than that ye have received, let him be accursed (1:6-9, KJV).

The afore mentioned methods in this chapter are later adaptations or inventions as they attempted to alter the teachings of the apostles as the same done with the Didache which by meaning is "Teaching" and is the short name of a Christian manual compiled before 300AD. Below you will notice an excerpt from the Didache that discusses baptism as it gives options outside of what taught in the Bible.

Chapter 7. Concerning Baptism

And concerning baptism, baptize this way: Having first said all these things, baptize into the name of the Father, and of the Son, and of the Holy Spirit, Matthew 28:19 in living water. But if you have not living water, baptize into other water; and if you can not in cold, in warm. But if you have not either, pour out water thrice upon the head into the name of Father and Son and Holy Spirit. But before the baptism let the baptizer fast, and the baptized, and whatever others can; but you shall order the baptized to fast one or two days before.[4]

This is a prime example of how error began to mount up in the church along with the Roman Catholic church making concessions that they have the right to not only interpret but to create doctrine because they felt they are the next power on earth under GOD.

The Vatican Council which met in Rome, in 1870, defined the doctrine of the infallibility of the Pope as follows:

"…We teach and define that it is a dogma divinely revealed that the Roman Pontiff, when he speaks ex cathedra, that is, when in discharge of the office of pastor and doctor of all Christians, by virtue of his supreme Apostolic authority, he defines a doctrine regarding faith and morals to be held by the

UNIVERSAL CHURCH, BY THE DIVINE ASSISTANCE PROMISED HIM IN BLESSED PETER, IS POSED OF THAT INFALLIBILITY…"[5]

When Nicodemus came to JESUS by night and inquired of him, JESUS did not say believe and though shall be saved, he didn't say confess with your mouth, and you shall be saved; he did not have Nicodemus to say the sinner's prayer, he informed Nicodemus that he must be born again of the water and the spirit. JESUS never deviated because in Mark 16:16, Matthew 28:19, and Luke 24:47 he gave the same instructions and the apostles carried out those same instructions throughout the book of Acts.

There is only one method that JESUS commissioned the apostles to teach concerning the new birth experience. I heard a couple of extremely popular preachers say on national television that there are many ways to GOD. One even went to the extent of using John 10:16, which states, "And other sheep I have, which are not of this fold: them also I must bring, and they shall hear my voice; and there shall be one-fold, and one shepherd (KJV)." This scripture is pre-church or New Covenant, and the audience to who JESUS is speaking is Jewish. John 10:16 precedes the verse that discusses how he will lay down his life, and therefore, the sheep he is speaking about is the pre-determined Body of Christ as the New Covenant church that will come into his fold. The Jews were upset at JESUS' speech, but the point was this is not a scripture that supports that there are many ways to GOD or other methods that can produce salvation.

What is consistent through scripture is listed in the chart, that everyone would "Heard the gospel," "Believe & Repent," "Be baptized," and "Receive the Holy Spirit." This is irrefutable based on Acts 2:37-44 for the Jews, Acts 8:5-17 for the Samaritans, Acts 10:33 we are all here in the presence of God; Acts 10:44-48 for the Gentiles, and Acts 18:24-28; Acts 19:1-5 for those who already are believers. It boils down to complete obedience to our LORD and Savior Jesus, who asks the question to all believers, "If ye love me, keep my commandments (John 14:15, KJV)."

CHAPTER 19 THE PROSPERITY GOSPEL

Miseducation: God wants the believer to live in financial prosperity.

---

3 John 1:2 Beloved, I wish above all things that thou mayest prosper and be in health, even as thy soul prospereth. (KJV)

In this chapter, we will discuss how the prosperity gospel is not a gospel at all. The prosperity gospel is also known as the Word of Faith movement or charismatic movement and was popularized by the late Oral Roberts. Those who preach such a message is described in John 10:12, "But he that is an hireling, and not the shepherd (KJV)." The message of prosperity has swindled so many people and has made a mockery of the church of the Living GOD. I listed above the scripture in 3 John 1:2 because I heard so many prosperity preachers use this to support their message of deceit. 3 John 1:2 is an epistle, which is a letter from John to his beloved friend Gaius and in his greeting, he just wished that he would prosper and be in good health as his soul is prospering. This is not a doctrine to the church even though it is used for our learning the greeting is a personal greeting to Gaius and not that everyone in the church is supposed to prosper because that would negate the fact that JESUS said in John 12:8 that "For the poor always ye have with you; but me ye have not always (KJV)."

Preaching for Money

Preaching a gospel that is motivated by raising substantial amounts of money is fraudulent to make false teachers wealthy. Paul said to the Galatian church, "I marvel that ye are so soon removed from him that called you into the grace of Christ unto another gospel: Which is not another; but there be some that trouble you, and would pervert the gospel of Christ (Gal 1:6-7, KJV). When I think of the prosperity preachers today, I think of the indulgence preachers of the Roman Catholic church. "On October 31, 1517, Martin Luther posted his Ninety-five Theses against papal indulgences, or the atonement of sins through monetary payment, on the door of the church at Wittenberg, Germany."[1] There is nowhere in scripture that preachers were invited to preach and there was an expected honorarium granted to preachers, nor was there any record in the Bible that described church assemblies raising offerings for a preacher or having lines of people waiting to give money or throw money at the altar. These methods are from charlatans and false preachers. Listen to what Paul informed the young pastor, Timothy, "This is a true saying, if a man desire the office of a bishop, he desireth a good work. 2 A bishop then must be blameless, the husband of one wife, vigilant, sober, of good behaviour, given to hospitality, apt to teach; 3 Not given to wine, no striker, not greedy of **filthy lucre**; but patient, not a brawler, not covetous; …8 Likewise must the deacons be grave, not doubletongued, not given to much wine, not greedy of **filthy lucre;** (1 Timothy 3:1-3,8, KJV). Paul also instructed Titus of the same, stating, "For a bishop must be blameless, as the steward of God; not selfwilled, not soon angry, not given to wine, no striker, not given to **filthy lucre;** Whose mouths must be stopped, who subvert whole houses, teaching things which they ought not, for **filthy lucre's sake** (Titus 1: 7,11, KJV)." This is the same message echoed by Peter in 1 Peter 5:2, saying, "Feed the flock of God, which is among you, taking the oversight thereof, not by constraint, but willingly; not for **filthy lucre,** but of a ready mind (KJV). When you look at the example that the apostles set for the church in the beginning, it looks nothing like today's church. Let us look at the first time money was distributed in the Body of Christ:

> *Acts 2:43-47 And fear came upon every soul: and many wonders and signs were done by the apostles. 44 And **all that believed were together, and had all things common**; 45 And **sold their possessions and goods, and parted them to all men, as every man had need.** 46 And they, continuing daily with one accord in the temple, and breaking bread from house to house, did eat their meat with gladness and singleness of heart, 47 Praising God, and having favour with all the people. And the Lord added to the church daily such as should be saved. (KJV)*

> *Acts 4:33-35 And with great power gave the apostles witness of the resurrection of the Lord Jesus: and great grace was upon them all. 34 Neither was there any among them that lacked: for as many as were possessors of lands or houses sold them, and brought the prices of the things that were sold, 35 And laid them down at the apostles' feet: and **distribution was made***

> *unto every man according as he had need.*
> *(KJV)*

Notice what the apostles did. After they preached with power and demonstration, it led people to believe, and many sold their lands and houses and brought the money to the apostles. The apostles did not buy themselves a big luxurious house, a top-of-the-line vehicle, a private jet, or anything to brandish themselves with materialistic things. They took the money and spread it to all the believers who had a need so everyone in the Body of Christ could have all things in common with nothing lacking. This is not the church today. Today, the church is caught up in capitalism, and preachers exploit the poor. You have preachers that are intemperate with their clothing, vehicles, homes, and other world possessions, while some members can barely pay their bills and have a decent meal or afford transportation to get to church.

Acquisition of Materialistic Gain

> *Romans 14:17 For the kingdom of God is not meat and drink; but righteousness, and peace, and joy in the Holy Ghost. (Rom 14:17 KJV)*

The mere motivation of these prosperity preachers is to acquire materialistic gain. These preachers will say that if you do not have enough faith to come out of your financial woes, then you need to strengthen your faith or speak it into existence. Other terms they use are manifest it, speak it, and believe it, and name it and claim it. Preachers who seek money will eventually be torn in two because "No one can serve two masters, for either he will hate the one and love the other, or he will be devoted to the one and despise the other. You cannot serve God and money (Mat 6:24 NET)." These preachers will make it seem as if something is wrong with you if you allow yourself to live in poverty or below a living wage when in 2020, there are 42.31 million people in the U.S. that live in poverty, and 44% do not make a living wage. The Bible instructs the Christian believer exactly what to do when encountering a preacher who equates gain with godliness. 1 Timothy 6:5 states, "Perverse disputings of men of corrupt minds, and destitute of the truth, **supposing that gain is godliness: from such withdraw thyself.** 6 But godliness with contentment is great gain. 7 For we brought nothing into this world, and it is certain we can carry nothing out. 8 And having food and raiment let us be therewith content. 9 But they that will be rich fall into temptation and a snare, and into many foolish and hurtful lusts, which drown men in destruction and perdition. 10 For the love of money is the root of all evil: which while some coveted after, they have erred from the faith and pierced themselves through with many sorrows. 11 But thou, O man of God, flee these things; and follow after righteousness, godliness, faith, love, patience, meekness. (1Ti 6:5-11, KJV)." In verse five, it instructs the believer to get away from them! However, people have equated materialistic gain with people having favor with GOD when that is not the case because the scriptures "Fret not thyself because of evildoers, neither be thou envious against the workers of iniquity. For they shall soon be cut down like the grass, and wither as the green herb (Ps 37:1-2, KJV)." Also, "Labour not to be rich: cease from thine own wisdom "Ps 23:4, KJV)." To drive the point even further Paul mentions to the church in Philippi "Not that I speak in respect of want: for I have learned, in whatsoever state I am, therewith to be content. I know both how to be abased, and I know how to abound: every where and in all things I am instructed both to be full and to be hungry, both to abound and to suffer need (Phil 4:11-12, KJV)."

Sowing a Seed...

Sowing a seed is another ploy of the prosperity preacher. This is one of those phrases that is usually one-sided. The prosperity preacher's whole concept behind this is sowing the seed into them so the parishioner can be blessed. I have yet to see this method work but in the favor of the preacher. Oral Roberts stated, "To realize your potential, to overcome life's problems, to see your life become fruitful, multiply and provide abundance (i.e., health, prosperity, spiritual renewal, in the family or oneself), you should decide to follow the divine law of the sower and the harvest. Sow the seed of His promise in the ground of your need" (from "Principles of the Seed").[2] These preachers would pervert scriptures like Luke 6:38, which states, "Give, and it shall be given unto you; good measure, pressed down, and shaken together, and running over, shall men give into your bosom. For with the same measure that ye mete withal it shall be measured to you again (KJV)." However, the problem is, if these prosperity preachers genuinely believed what they were teaching, they would be the ones who would be sowing the seeds of money into the people and not have the people emptying their pockets and bank accounts to bless the preacher so they can be blessed. There is nothing wrong with asking the LORD for something as long as they have; I mind James 1:6, which says, "But let him ask in faith, nothing wavering. For he, that wavereth is like a wave of the sea driven with the wind and tossed. 7 For let not that man think that he shall receive any thing of the Lord. (Jam. 1:6 KJV)." These false teachers would conjure up ploys to make money to the extent of selling items on their television broadcast as if it is a home shopping network or a telethon just to build their own personal kingdom.

Another scripture they will use without quoting the entire text in an attempt to manipulate the believers is James 4:2-3. What they will usually say is, "you have not because you ask not." This is a small part of the end of the scripture in James 4:2 but what it really says is, "Ye lust, and have not: ye kill, and desire to have, and cannot obtain: ye fight and war, yet ye have not, because ye ask not. Ye ask, and receive not, because ye ask amiss, that ye may consume it upon your lusts (Jam 4:2-3 KJV)." The scripture has nothing to do with someone not having something because they simply do not ask GOD. What it is saying is that you are not having because your motivation of asking was lustful or an evil desire and that you ask amiss or as for something that is out of the desire of GOD.

Another scripture that these false teachers will misinterpret is Matthew 6:33, which states, "But seek ye first the kingdom of God, and his righteousness; and all these things shall be added unto you (KJV)." They will teach this as if it means that if you seek the kingdom of GOD, then you can receive all the things you desire. This is a cheap interpretation because it lacks context. All in verse 33 does not mean everything; it means everything that the previous verses were talking about. To gain a better context we will read the earlier two verses as it says, "Therefore take no thought, saying, What shall we **eat**? or, What shall we **drink**? or, Wherewithal shall we be **clothed**? 32 (For after all these things do the Gentiles seek:) for your heavenly Father knoweth that ye have need of all these things. 33 But seek ye first the kingdom of God, and his righteousness, and all these things shall be added unto you (KJV)." This text is clearly discussing the basic necessities of life, which is eating, drinking, and being clothes. It is not talking about the acquisition of materialistic gain.

Money Means Nothing

Earthly riches have no heavenly value. Luke 14:14 states, "and thou shalt be blessed; for they cannot recompense thee: for thou shalt be recompensed at the resurrection of the just (KJV)." JESUS is clear in his teaching that earthly currency has no meaning when comparing it to heavenly matters. In fact, it is discouraged by JESUS because Matthew 19:23-26 states, "Then said Jesus unto his disciples, Verily I say unto you, That a rich man shall hardly enter into the kingdom of heaven. And again, I say unto you, It is easier for a camel to go through the eye of a needle, than for a rich man to enter into the kingdom of God. When his disciples heard it, they were exceedingly amazed, saying, Who then can be saved? But Jesus beheld them, and said unto them, With men this is impossible; but with God all things are possible (KJV)." This was very discouraging to the disciples, but JESUS didn't say you couldn't be wealthy rather, it is just a challenge to be rich and make it into eternal life, for this is the reason Paul told Timothy the reason by stating, "But they that will be rich fall into temptation and a snare, and into many foolish and hurtful lusts, which drown men in destruction and perdition (1 Tim 6:9-10, KJV)."

Living in a materialistic world, many think that money is valuable. It has value but only to man and earthly things, which will eventually decay, and the moths and worms will eat up, or it will rust away and cannot last. This is why Matthew 6:19 states, "Lay not up for yourselves treasures upon earth, where moth and rust doth corrupt, and where thieves break through and steal: (KJV)." I am reminded of the story in Acts 8:18-20 "when Simon saw that through laying on of the apostles' hands the Holy Ghost was given, he offered them money, saying, give me also this power, that on whomsoever I lay hands, he may receive the Holy Ghost. But Peter said unto him, thy money perish with thee, because thou hast thought that the gift of God may be purchased with money (KJV)." Every preacher's conduct must be free from the love of money, and you must be content with what you have, for he has said, "I will never leave you, and I will never abandon you (Heb 13:5, NET)" and not a drunkard, not violent, but gentle, not contentious, free from the love of money. (1Tim. 3:3 NET) and a man's life should not consist in the abundance of the things which he possesses. (Luk 12:15)."

CHAPTER 20 COMMONLY MISINTERPRETED SCRIPTURES

1. **Proverbs 18:16** A man's gift maketh room for him, and bringeth him before great men. (KJV)

   This scripture does not mean that your spiritual gift will open doors for you, but it is bribery. This text describes a bribe. This is an old example of a quid pro quo, where an exchange of one person's gift will allow them to get in the presence of powerful men and give you a seat at the table. The Hebrew term translated "gift" is a more general term than "bribe" (שֹׁחַד, shokhad), used in 17:8, 23. But it also has danger (e.g., 15:27; 21:14), for by giving gifts one might learn how influential they are and use them for bribes. The proverb simply says that a gift can expedite matters. (ref. NET footnote on Proverbs 18:16)

2. **Isaiah 10:27** And it shall come to pass in that day, that his burden shall be taken away from off thy shoulder, and his yoke from off thy neck, and the yoke shall be destroyed because of the anointing.

   Many preachers will use this scripture to say it is the anointing that destroys the yoke in an over-spiritualized expression when, in actuality, it is discussing how the LORD as the Good Shepherd will feed you to the extent that you will grow extremely large to the extent that your neck will become so large that the yoke will break off. The NET translation brings more clarity as it says, "At that time the Lord will remove their burden from your shoulders, and their yoke from your neck the yoke will be taken off because your neck will be too large (Is 10:27, NET)."

"The meaning of this line is uncertain. The Hebrew text reads, "and the yoke will be destroyed (or "pulled down") because of fatness." This is a bizarre picture of an ox growing so large that it breaks the yoke around its neck or can no longer fit into its yoke. Fatness would symbolize the Lord's restored blessings; the removal of the yoke would symbolize the cessation of Assyrian oppression. Because of the difficulty of the metaphor, many prefer to emend the text at this point. Some emend וְחֻבַּל (vekhubbal, "and it will be destroyed," a perfect with prefixed vav), to יְחֻבַּל (yikhbol, "[it] will be destroyed," an imperfect), and take the verb with what precedes, "and their yoke will be destroyed from your neck." Proponents of this view (cf. NAB, NRSV) then emend עֹל ('ol, "yoke") to עָלָה ('alah, "he came up") and understand this verb as introducing the following description of the Assyrian invasion (vv. 28-32). מִפְּנֵי שָׁמֶן (mippeney shamen, "because of fatness") is then amended to read "from before Rimmon" (NAB, NRSV), "from before Samaria," or "from before Jeshimon." Although this line may present difficulties, it regards best line as a graphic depiction of God's abundant blessings on his servant nation." (ref. NET footnote on Isaiah 10:27)

3. **Isaiah 53:5** But he was wounded for our transgressions, he was bruised for our iniquities: the chastisement of our peace was upon him; and with his stripes we are healed (Isa 53:5 KJV)."

   Most people have interpreted this text as scripture that includes physical healing and is commonly used by preachers when praying for people that has physical infirmities. However, this is a text that is considered a Hebrew parallel, which means it is repetitive in nature due to the poetic style of the Hebrew language. This scripture is only speaking of the healing of sin and nothing more, and the scripture that confirms this is 1 Peter 2:24, which states, "Who his own self bare our sins in his own body on the tree, that we, being dead to sins, should live unto righteousness: by whose stripes ye were healed (KJV)." In Isaiah 53:5, the phrase "with his stripes we are healed" is repeated by Peter in 1 Peter 2:24 and identifies what the healing is for which is sin. That exact phrase in Isaiah 53:5 is preceded by why he was wounded and bruised, which is sin described as transgressions and iniquities.

4. **Matthew 6:33** "But seek ye first the kingdom of God, and his righteousness; and all these things shall be added unto you (KJV)."

   Many preachers will teach this as if it means that if you seek the kingdom of GOD, then you can receive all the things you desire. This is a cheap interpretation because it lacks context. All in verse thirty-three does not mean everything; it means everything that the previous verses were talking about. To gain a better context we will reach the earlier two verses as it says, "Therefore take no thought, saying, What shall we eat? or, What shall we drink? or, Wherewithal shall we be clothed? 32 (For after all these things do the Gentiles seek:) for your heavenly Father knoweth that ye have need of all these things. 33 But seek ye first the kingdom of God, and his righteousness and all these things shall be added unto you (KJV)." This text is clearly discussing the basic necessities of life, which is eating, drinking, and being clothes. It is not talking about the acquisition of materialistic gain.

5. **Matthew 7:7** Ask, and it shall be given you; seek, and ye shall find; knock, and it shall be opened unto you. (KJV)

Many have used this scripture in ways that is beyond its intended meaning. The most common error in interpreting this text is that it illudes to a meaning of persistence in prayer. Some has even gone to the extreme to teach that it means the three stages of prayers that you first ask, then seek, and finally knock. The reason this is incorrect is because in the synoptic gospel of Luke's version gives a fuller understanding of what the subject matter is concerning in this text. In Luke 11:9-13 9 And I say unto you, Ask, and it shall be given you; seek, and ye shall find; knock, and it shall be opened unto you. 10 For every one that asketh receiveth; and he that seeketh findeth; and to him that knocketh it shall be opened. 11 If a son shall ask bread of any of you that is a father, will he give him a stone? or if he ask a fish, will he for a fish give him a serpent? 12 Or if he shall ask an egg, will he offer him a scorpion? 13 If ye then, being evil, know how to give good gifts unto your children: how much more shall your heavenly Father give the Holy Spirit to them that ask him? Luke explains that this text is the understanding of the LORD's intentions to give His believers the gift of the Holy Spirit when asking by using a Hebrew parallel to explain it. The Hebrew parallel is a way of explaining something by using two or more lines that are synonymous or have a close correlation with one another in order to be emphatic. In this case, it uses the words ask, seek, and knock.

6. **Matthew 16:19** And I will give unto thee the keys of the kingdom of heaven: and whatsoever thou shalt bind on earth shall be bound in heaven: and whatsoever thou shalt loose on earth shall be loosed in heaven (KJV).

The key to understanding how to interpret Matthew 16:19 is in the words bound and loosed. The word bound is from the Greek word δεδεμένον which is a perfect passive verb as well as λελυμένον. When interpreting a perfect passive verb, it must be understood as an ACTION COMPLETED at a SPECIFIC POINT of TIME in PAST with results CONTINUING into the PRESENT. In certain contexts, the results are PERMANENT. With this in mind, when reading Matthew 16:19 it should be interpreted as, "And I will give unto thee the keys of the kingdom of heaven: and whatsoever thou shalt bind on earth should have already been bound in heaven: and whatsoever thou shalt loose on earth should have already been loosed in heaven." This scripture is not meant to be understood as whatsoever is bound on earth will then be bound in heaven as a chain reaction. It is teaching us that what Jesus did on the cross has allowed Christians to exercise a certain amount of authority and power, and when we align ourselves up to the order of heaven, then the things that have been ordained for Christians will be in instant effect because they are already done!

7. **Romans 4:17** (As it is written, I have made thee a father of many nations,) before him whom he believed, even God, who quickeneth the dead, and calleth those things which be not as though they were.

Many professing believers will use this scripture to encourage other believers to call things that are not into existence and will encourage them to speak things into existence. This belief has no origin in Christianity; however, it has entered into it from New Ageism, Hinduism, and astrophysics. This scripture clearly is saying that it is GOD and HIM only that can bring the dead alive and call things into reality that are not a reality or bring things into existence that do not exist. This interpretation is suiting in giving a reference to God's creative power.

8. **Romans 5:20** Moreover the law entered, that the offence might abound. But where sin abounded, grace did much more abound: (Rom 5:20 KJV)

This text is used by proponents of the belief that "Once saved always saved or eternal security. This has been interpreted that if a believer has sinned then no matter how great the sin, grace would rise to the extent of the sin to cover it. It is true that if a believer sins, they can "confess their sins and he is faithful and just to forgive us our sins, and to cleanse us from all unrighteousness (1 Jn 1:9, KJV)." However, Romans 5:20 has been used as a license to sin and be presumptuous about their sinful acts as grace would continue to cover it. This is what is considered antinomianism, which means that since Christians are saved by grace then they can live however they want to live because of grace. This a strict contradiction to Romans 6:1, which says, "What shall we say then? Shall we continue in sin, that grace may abound (KJV)?" The book of Jude discusses how there were evil men who sneaked into the church and were turning the grace of our God into lasciviousness (1:4). This means using grace as a license to sin. Even the Psalmist in 19:13 prayed, "keep back thy servant also from presumptuous sins (KJV)."

9. **Ephesians 2:8** For by grace are ye saved through faith; and that not of yourselves: it is the gift of God: (Eph 2:8 KJV)

This text is usually used to support the idea that we are saved by faith as opponents of legalism or being saved by works. "The problem is that people are reading into this text their own personal interpretation and are not considering the other scriptures that deal with salvation, and they equate things like baptism a work. First, baptism is not considered a work in the scripture. Works are clearly described in the book of James 2:14-26. Primarily works are described as deeds or good deeds toward others in James 2:15. But for the sake of conversation, then we will look at baptism as a work, and if so, then we will read, "17 So also faith of itself, if it does not have works, is dead. 20 Do you want proof, you ignoramus, that faith without works is useless? 24 You see that a man is justified by works, and not by faith alone (NABRE)." To use an analogy to explain the meaning of the scripture in Ephesians 2:8 would be: If a person is on top a 10-story building that is on fire and the only choice is to jump and the fire department brings a net to place at the bottom of the building in the direction of the person. If the person decides to jump, what saves the person, the jump, or the net? Obviously, the net saved the man because if it were not a net there the person would be able to survive the impact of the ground. In this analogy, grace is the net, and faith is the jump. Leaving your former life is always a leap of faith; however, if you do not have the grace of GOD to catch you, then there is no saving.

10. **Hebrews 11:1** Now faith is the substance of things hoped for, the evidence of things not seen. (Heb 11:1 KJV)

The word "now" in this text is a conjunction that could also be read as faith... However, I have heard preachers use the word "now" as an adverb of time as if it means we need some right now faith or some present-time faith, at this moment, or very soon. This is another case of eisegesis, meaning reading into the scripture your own personal interpretation and not giving the true interpretation of the text.

11. **James 4:2** Ye lust, and have not: ye kill, and desire to have, and cannot obtain: ye fight and war, yet ye have not, because ye ask not. (KJV)

Most people will misinterpret this scripture and take it out of context because they would not quote the scripture in its entirety. Many would only quote the last few words of the text and say, "You have not because you ask not." This is taking a part of James 4:2 out of context. By doing this, it gives a new meaning that was not intended. This is usually said to many believers with the misleading thought process that you don't have because you don't ask, and if you ask God, he will give it to you. This is an error because the scripture is alluding to the fact that people ask for things with the wrong motives, and therefore, they do not receive. They do not ask according to the LORD's will they ask according to their will or their lust. In 1 John 5:14, it says, "And this is the confidence that we have in him, that, if we ask any thing according to his will, he heareth us." Also, to understand James 4:2 the reader needs to take in the whole thought to understand the context. James 4:2-3 in the NAS translation says, "You lust and do not have; so, you commit murder. And you are envious and cannot obtain so, you fight and quarrel. You do not have because you do not ask. You ask and do not receive, because you ask with wrong motives, so that you may spend it on your pleasures.

12. **1 John 5:7** For there are three that bear record in heaven, the Father, the Word, and the Holy Ghost: and these three are one. (1Jo 5:7 KJV)

There is no Greek text that supports this translation. The Greek text for 1 John 5:7 is rendered "ὅτι τρεῖς εἰσιν οἱ μαρτυροῦντες, (SBLT)." These five Greek words could not be translated as the English version, but in the NET translation it is correct as it is translated as "For there are three that testify."

13. **3 John 1:2** Beloved, I wish above all things that thou mayest prosper and be in health, even as thy soul prospereth. (KJV)

3 John 1:2 is an epistle, a letter from John to his beloved friend Gaius and in his greeting, he just wished that he would prosper and be in good health as his soul is prospering. This is not a doctrine to the church even though it is used for our learning the greeting is a personal greeting to Gaius and not that everyone in the church is

supposed to prosper because that would negate the fact that JESUS said in John 12:8 that, "For the poor always ye have with you; but me ye have not always (KJV)."

14. When praises go up then blessings come down. **(NOT A SCRIPTURE!!!)**

This one phrase has been popularized in charismatic circles and used to incite emotionalism, as if it is supposed to ignite an automatic eruption of GOD's blessing if everyone begins to praise GOD. You cannot find this in the Bible, even though many would claim it is valid due to experience.

15. The race is not given to the swift, nor the battle to the strong but he that endures to the end shall be saved. **(NOT A SCRIPTURE!!!)**

People who use this phrase are really combining different scriptures together, and it has been a common saying among churchgoers. The first part of the saying comes from Ecclesiastes 9:11 "I returned, and saw under the sun, that **the race is not to the swift, nor the battle to the strong,** neither yet bread to the wise, nor yet riches to men of understanding, nor yet favour to men of skill; but time and chance happeneth to them all (KJV)." The next part of the saying comes from Matthew 24:13 13 But he that shall endure unto the end, the same shall be saved (KJV)."

CHAPTER 21 IDEX OF UNBIBLICAL WORDS AND MISUSED BIBLICAL WORDS

1. **Accept Christ:** Accepting Christ is a common phrase among churches. This term is used as a mode of salvation or confession of the belief that one has entered fellowship with Christ. This term is incorrect due to the scripture teaches that "But as many as received him, to them gave he power to become the sons of God, *even* to them that believe on his name: (Joh 1:12 KJV)." However, Ephesians 1:6 states, "To the praise of the glory of his grace, wherein he hath made us accepted in the beloved (KJV)." We do not accept Christ He accepts us, but we do have the opportunity to receive Him.

2. **Armor Bearer:** Have you wondered why preachers will bring their Bible to the church but need someone to carrier their Bible to the pulpit? Armor bearer is an Old Testament concept where soldiers would have an armor bearer to carry their armor to battle because the armor was made of heavy metals, and the journey to battle would be a great distance. To prevent extreme fatigue before battle, an armor bearer was needed. In the Old Testament, the term armor bearer is obsolete. However, ministers today would give the title out to individuals for them to be servants or companions to aid them. This is not

the Biblical description of an armor bearer. In the book of Ephesians chapter six, it is commanded to the believer to "put on the whole armor of God," and it was not to be taken off at any time. An armor bearer is not someone who carries another person's Bible to the pulpit.

3. **Ash Wednesday:** Ash Wednesday is not a Biblical practice, nor was it practiced by the 1st-century church. According to the Catholic Encyclopedia, it is the first day of the observance of the 40 days of Lent. It takes its name from the solemn ceremony of the liturgy of the day wherein the ashes of palms or other suitable substances are blessed and then marked on the foreheads of the faithful in the form of a cross with the accompanying words, "Remember, man, you are dust and to dust you shall return." Or: "Repent and believe the Good News." It is thus a solemn call to penance so that one may enjoy eternal life. It was established as the first day of Lent by St. Gregory the Great (590 to 604). Pope Paul VI declared this moveable observance in the Church calendar to be a day of universal fasting and abstinence.[1]

4. **Christmas:** Puritans forbade Christmas, considering it too pagan. Governor Bradford actually threatened New Englanders with work, jail, or fines if they were caught observing Christmas. In 1659, the Massachusetts Bay Colony enacted a law called Penalty for Keeping Christmas. The notion

was that such "festivals as were superstitiously kept in other countries" were a "great dishonor of God and offense of others." Anyone found celebrating Christmas by not working, "feasting, or any other way... shall pay for every such offense five shillings.[2] These sentiments as far spread past New England but also in England. Many believe that the celebration of Christmas aligned itself with the date of birth for the pagan god Horus, but there is much debate. However, "In ancient Rome, December 25 was a celebration of the Unconquered Sun, marking the return of longer days. It followed Saturnalia, a festival where people feasted and exchanged gifts. The church in Rome began celebrating Christmas on December 25 in the 4th century during the reign of Constantine, the first Christian emperor, possibly to weaken pagan traditions."[3] No matter the debate, the fact is that Christmas did not find its roots in Biblical customs nor did the 1st century church celebrate a holiday that was remotely close to Christmas. According to Roman Catholic tradition, Christmas is when they are allowed to have three masses in observance of the holiday. This is where the name comes from Christ's mass.

5. **Covering:** What is a covering? Is covering a Biblical term? The word covering is in the Bible, so it is Biblical; however, it is used out of context in the Christian church today. Pastors will inform believers that they need a covering, implying that the Pastor is the believer's covering. Although this is not a bad concept,

what is a spiritual covering? Does a person or minister need a covering?

Most Christians who adhere to spiritual coverings believe they should be accountable not only to God but also to a spiritual leader. This earthly authority figure serves as an intercessor and, in extreme cases, as a substitute for God in the life of the person being "covered."

Supporters look to verses such as 1 Thessalonians 5:12–13, 1 Corinthians 11:2–16, and 1 Peter 5:5 as biblical backing for spiritual covering. However, in practice, the line between God's authority and a spiritual shepherd can easily blur.

The practice of spiritual covering can lead to spiritual, emotional, and other abuses. Some early advocates, such as Bob Mumford and Charles Simpson, now distance themselves from the idea and have apologized for their involvement. The idea itself is not completely without merit; however, the practice of spiritual covering lends itself to difficulties.

Spiritual covering is often referred to in connection with the Shepherding movement. There it means that a Christian submits to the authority of another believer in a way that his or her spiritual life or ministry is valid to God only under direct supervision of this specific person. That person is usually an elder, pastor, or older, more mature Christian. The idea that another human validates spiritual life or ministry is not biblical. Though initially developed within the charismatic movement, the spiritual covering is now associated with the New Apostolic

Reformation, some Messianic Judaism, and the Hebrew Roots movement.

Submission, of course, is biblical. Submission to God is necessary. Additionally, Romans 13:1 instructs Christians to respect authority; Ephesians 5:21 instructs believers in mutual submission; John 13:34 instructs Christians about loving one another. As for an individual's submission to another, looking to the experience and wisdom of others just makes sense. It is when that practice is mandated with authority that it begins to erode any legitimate practice of spiritual covering.

As Christians, we are only accountable to God (Romans 3:19; Matthew 12:36). We should consult with others for advice (Proverbs 11:14) and learn from others humbly (Proverbs 5:11–14). We look to God for approval, not men (2 Timothy 2:15). Our service to God is not validated by any person (Romans 14:4), and mandating individual authority within an organization or church can harm a person's relationship with Jesus (1 Timothy 2:5) and can cause division within the church (1 Corinthians 3:4–9). Jesus spoke about authority in Matthew 20:25–28: "But Jesus called them to him and said, 'You know that the rulers of the Gentiles lord it over them, and their great ones exercise authority over them. It shall not be so among you. But whoever would be great among you must be your servant, and whoever would be first among you must be your slave, even as the Son of Man came not to be served but to serve, and to give his life as a ransom for many." (https://www.compellingtruth.org/spiritual-covering.html)

6. **Denomination:** Denomination is not a Biblical term but an arithmetic term that means division. Denominationalism comes from differences of belief and teachings, and this is the premise and embodiment of why there is confusion among Christian believers. When denominations are formed it is usually because doctrines are not viewed through rightly dividing the word of GOD but by the cultural context of individuals. Often, they are formed out of pride and the lack of spiritual integrity, and from the errors of interpretation, many sects are started. Other reasons for the divisions stem from theological disagreements, doctrinal disputes, power and authority struggles, disagreements in worship and liturgical practices, social change and cultural divides, missions and direction of the ministry, and other schisms. Below is a list of some denominations to name a few:
    - Anglicanism
    - Baptist
    - Catholicism/Catholic
    - Mormon/ Church of the Latter-Day Saints
    - Amish
    - Anabaptist
    - Church of Christ
    - Episcopal
    - Greek Orthodox
    - Seventh Day Adventist
    - Jehovah Witness

- Pentecostal
- Protestant
- Presbyterian
- Puritans
- Lutheran
- Quakerism (Society of Friends)
- Reformed Church
- Methodist (C.M.E, A.M.E, U.M.E, A.M.E. Zion)

7. **Doors of the Church are Open:** The phrase, "the doors of the church are open" sometimes referred to as the "altar call" cannot be traced to an origin or denomination but is used at the end of most traditional protestant churches at the transition into the portion of the service that allows the attendees to come to the altar for prayer or participate in the rituals of becoming born again. The ushers and attendees open the doors of the church building and continue to the altar. This phrase has no Biblical precedent because at the time of Christ's triumph over death and the grave He gave access for believers to enter the kingdom of God when the veil was rent at the temple during His crucifixion. Therefore, the doors of the church were opened at Calvary when the blood of JESUS was shed for the remission of sin. The doors of the church not only were opened at Calvary, but nobody closed it then, nor can anyone close it now. For this reason, there is no need to say, "The doors of the church are open" in a Christian service. In Romans 5:2 we have access by faith into this grace wherein we stand, in Ephesians 2:18 we both have access by in one Spirit to

the Father, in Ephesians 3:12 we have boldness and access with confidence by the faith of him, and in Revelation 22:14 we have access to the tree of life and can enter the city by the gates.

8. **Drunk in the spirit/Slain in the spirit:** This phrase is a term that derives from a misinterpretation of scripture as well as a description of emotionalism when a person identifies with a Pentecostal experience. The scripture used in error is Acts 2:13-15 "Others mocking said, these men are full of new wine. But Peter, standing up with the eleven, lifted up his voice, and said unto them, Ye men of Judaea, and all ye that dwell at Jerusalem, be this known unto you, and hearken to my words: For these are not drunken, as ye suppose, seeing it is but the third hour of the day (KJV)." The outpouring of the Holy Spirit resulted in the repented believers speaking in different languages they were not trained to speak. This phenomenon was so amazing that some were astonished, and some mocked them. Peter simply explained the mockery away. From this scripture, believers who have claimed to receive the same experience in their zeal, but lack of knowledge began to describe their actions as being drunk in the spirit. Drunkenness is an unseemly action, and the Holy Spirit does not behave itself unseemly.

9. **Easter:** The word Easter shows up in the Bible in the KJV in Acts 12:4 where it states, "And when he had

apprehended him, he put him in prison, and delivered him to four quaternions of soldiers to keep him; intending after Easter to bring him forth to the people (KJV)." However, the King James Version in the book of Acts 12:4 is the only translation that uses the word Easter in place of the Greek word "πάσχα" which is translated as Passover. Easter and Passover are not the same thing. Passover comes from the Hebrew word "pe·saḥ פֶּסַח" from the Exodus story of chapter 12 about the Passover Lamb. "The English word Easter, which parallels the German word Ostern, is of uncertain origin. One view, expounded by the Venerable Bede in the 8th century, was that it derived from Eostre, or Eostrae, the Anglo-Saxon goddess of spring and fertility. This view presumes—as does the view associating the origin of Christmas on December 25 with pagan celebrations of the winter solstice—that Christians appropriated pagan names and holidays for their highest festivals."[3] Although no one can validate the origin of Easter as a pagan goodness or festival, we do know for sure that it was not a practice of the 1st-century church, nor was it a Biblical custom to celebrate JESUS' death and resurrection with painted eggs and rabbits.

10. **Eternal Son:** Eternal Son is a made-up title to describe a believe that the son of GOD was always with GOD from eternity and took part with GOD in all of the creative works and human influence. If this is the case, then this does strengthen the separate persons of GOD, and therefore, there is no monotheism in the Christian faith. The sonship had a particular purpose in the plan of GOD to be a sacrificial lamb, and therefore, the sonship has a beginning and an end. In Psalms 2:7; Heb 1:5; and Isaiah 9:6 speaks to the beginning of the sonship:

- *Psalm 2:7 I will declare the decree: the Lord hath said unto me, Thou art my Son; this day have I begotten thee. (KJV)*
- *Hebrews 1:5 For unto which of the angels said he at any time, Thou art my Son, this day have I begotten thee? And again, I will be to him a Father, and he shall be to me a Son? (KJV)*
- *Isaiah 9:6 For unto us a child is born, unto us a son is given: and the government shall be upon his shoulder: and his name shall be called Wonderful, Counsellor, The mighty God, The everlasting Father, The Prince of Peace. (KJV)*

Then in 1 Corinthians 15:24-28 speaks to the end of the sonship:

1 Corinthians 15:24-28

24 Then cometh the end, when he shall have delivered up the kingdom to God, even the Father; when he shall have put down all rule and all authority and power. 25 For he must reign, till he hath put all enemies under his feet. 26 The last enemy that shall be destroyed is death. 27 For he hath put all things under his feet. But when he saith all things are put under him, it is manifest that he is excepted, which did put all things under him. 28 And when all things shall be subdued unto him, then shall the Son also himself be subject unto him that put all things under him, that God may be all in all. (KJV)

11. **Eternal Security:** This is not a Biblical teaching and there are too many scriptures to ignore about the perseverance for this doctrine to be true. The doctrine of eternal security is a reformed doctrine whose champion is John Calvin. This doctrine holds to the sort of perseverance of the saints, according to which true Christians will persevere in good works and faith because faith is God's perfect gift, and it will inevitably produce salvation not requiring a life of holiness or Biblical morality. (Please see chapter 3)

12. **Fire Baptized:** Fire baptized has been used as a term to describe a believer that has been baptized with the Holy Spirit, however, no one wants to be baptized with fire as the Bible describes. In Matthew 3:11 it says, "I indeed baptize you with water unto repentance: but he that cometh after me is mightier than I, whose shoes I am not worthy to bear he shall

baptize you with the Holy Ghost, and with fire (KJV)." The Holy Spirit and fire are two separate baptisms. For in the next verse, it describes how "he will burn up the chaff with unquenchable fire." Fire baptism is when the earth is purified with fire to start anew. The Holy Spirit baptism is to save people from the fire baptism. Nevertheless, believers with zeal but lacking knowledge will use baptized with fire as an emotional response to receiving the power of the Holy Spirit and is in error associating Matthew 3:11 with Act 2:3 when it states, "there appeared unto them cloven tongues like as of fire" that the apostles experienced. That was not a baptism because baptism means to be fully submerged.

13. **Found God:** No one has ever found GOD because GOD has never been lost. People are lost and GOD finds them. Luke 19:10 For the Son of man is come to look for and to save that which was lost. (KJV)

14. **Holiness standards:** A set of rules that are imposed upon believers through their denomination that often are not Biblical or stem from misinterpreted scriptures.

15. **Join the Church:** No one can join the church because the church is not a fraternity, sorority, club, or organization; it is an organism. You must be born again to be a part of the church because the church is not a building; it is a spiritual adoption of

God. The new birth puts you in the family of God, and you become a child of the MOST HIGH GOD and a new creation.

16. **Lent:** Lent is another tradition that is not found in the Bible as a custom practiced or commanded by the first-century church. However, the practice is common among Catholics, Greek Orthodox, Lutherans, Anglicans, Episcopalians, Methodists, and others. Lenten traditions and practices have evolved over time, but it involves fasting for 40 days from Ash Wednesday to Easter. The earliest recordings of Lent appeared shortly following the Council of Nicea in 325 AD. It was Pope Gregory I (590 - 604) who finally regularized the period of the fast churchwide, to begin on a Wednesday 46 days before Easter with a ceremony of ash, and not to include Sundays, which were perennial days of celebration.[5]

17. **Personal Savior:** Personal savior is not a Biblical term or phrase but finds its roots in the idea that JESUS went to the cross just for individuals, and he knew them before they entered the world and knew the sins they were going to commit and therefore became their personal savior. This is contradictory because JESUS died for the sins of the world according to John 1:29 and whosoever believeth in him can have everlasting life according to John 3:16. He didn't have to die for our individual sins because there is nothing new under

the sun and he died for all sins that was committed or would be committed.

18. **Purgatory:** Purgatory cannot be found in the Bible as a doctrine of JESUS or the early church. This is purely a Catholic invention to manipulate believers to pay a penance to help get loved ones out of purgatory and into heaven. Defined by the Catholic Encyclopedia, purgatory is "the soul of those who have died in the state of grace suffer for a time a purging that prepares them to enter heaven and appear in the presence of the beatific vision. Thus, the purpose of purgatory is to cleanse one of imperfections, venial sins, and faults, and to remit or do away with the temporal punishments due to mortal sins that have been forgiven in the Sacrament of Penance. It is an intermediate state in which the departed souls can atone for unforgiven sins before receiving their final reward."

19. **The Sinner's Prayer:** The sinner's prayer is not a Biblical teaching for the process of the new birth. The sinner's prayer stood for a quick and easy way to deal with individual seekers during a large meeting to not bottle-neck the services and put salvation on microwave speed. It is, however, a novel approach to evangelism. My research shows that the Sinner's Prayer was not popularized until late into the twentieth

century, possibly as late as the 1940s or even the early 1950s. (See chapter 9 and chapter 18)

20. **Soul Ties:** The term "soul ties" has been taught by some preachers in the sense that after having intimate relationships with someone or many partners those individuals are connected to your soul and even though the LORD saves you, you still need to be delivered from the many souls that you entangled yourself with. This is a ridiculous teaching, and the proponents of it use Genesis 34:3, which says, "And his soul clave unto Dinah the daughter of Jacob, and he loved the damsel, and spake kindly unto the damsel (KJV)." This one scripture does not dictate a teaching that supports this theory. Once the LORD has delivered someone from the penalty of sins, then everyone still must go through the sanctification process of purging or dying to their fleshly inclinations. If a person feels that they suffer from a so-called "soul tie" then that is no more than that person needing to continue to be sanctified from their lustful desire of wanting to be with previous partners. Everybody's sanctification process is different, and therefore, everyone who has multiple partners does not have problems with the so-called teaching of "soul ties." In 2 Corinthians 5:17, it says, "Therefore if any man be in Christ, he is a new creature: old things are passed away; behold, all things are become new (KJV)."

21. **Titles of ministers out of various denominational organizations:**

    The titles listed below are used by various denominations within organizations and do not represent the various ministries that are used in the Bible.

    - Archbishop - (not in the Bible)
    - Cardinal - (not in the Bible)
    - Chief Apostle - (not in the Bible)
    - Ecumenical Patriarch - (not in the Bible)
    - Holy Father - (not in the Bible)
    - Lay minister – (not in the Bible)
    - Monk - (not in the Bible)
    - Parson - (not in the Bible)
    - Pope - (not in the Bible)
    - Priest – (all believers in GOD are priests, 1 Pet. 2:9)
    - Reverend – (only GOD name is Holy and inspires reverence, Ps. 111:9)
    - Saint (saint is not a title but we are called to be saints or holy even sanctified, Rom. 1:7, 1 Cor. 1:2)
    - Suffragan Bishop - (not in the Bible)
    - Superintendent - (not in the Bible)

    Technically, there are no titles for ministers in the Body of Christ, only descriptions of their job duties, assignments, or the office they occupy. The apostles of the LORD were not using the term apostle as a noun, they used it as an adjective. In the salutation of Paul's letters, it always referred to Paul as an apostle or servant, but it never referred to him as Apostle Paul. If you do not call modern ministers by their title, they will feel disrespected because of pride and they love the preeminence over people. The description of the ministry in the Bible is described in Ephesians 4:11, which says, "And he gave some, apostles; and some, prophets; and some, evangelists; and some, pastors and teachers; (KJV)." Also, in Acts 20:17,28 the elders of the church were assembled and charged to be overseers (bishops) over the church of GOD and to feed them. In 2 Corinthians 3:6, they are called able ministers of the New Testament; and in 1 Timothy chapter 3, the bishops were given a charge, and the deacons were to keep the same charge. Even when using proper descriptions of minister roles, there is a misuse of the office they serve in. For example, Bishops, Pastors, and Elders are separated in an organizational structure that derives from the Episcopal polity. In the Bible, they are the same according to Acts 20:17,28. The Elders were called to be overseers and to feed the church of God. The Greek word for overseer is ἐπίσκοπος (ep-is'-kop-os), which is translated as bishop later in church history, but the elder was a bishop. Also, the word feed comes from ποιμαίνω (poy-mah'-ee-no) derives from the root word ποιμήν (poy-mane') which means to shepherd or pastor. So, it is safe to say that every pastor is a bishop and does not need to run for a politically driven position in an organization because if a person is a true ordained by GOD pastor, then it is the same as a bishop and an elder. today are used as servants but in the Bible, they were just as important as the bishops. Another misused office today is the prophet. Today, the prophet is a typical hireling prophet who is more of a fortune teller. The Biblical prophets gave correction and instruction from GOD to the people, and furthermore, Revelation 19:10 says, "for the testimony of Jesus is the spirit of prophecy (KJV)." The greatest description of a minister in the Body of Christ is a servant.

> *Matthew 23:8-12 But you are not to be called 'Rabbi,' for you have one Teacher and you are all brothers. [9] And call no one your 'father' on earth, for you have one Father, who is in heaven. [10] Nor are you to be called 'teacher,' for you have one teacher, the Christ. [11] The greatest among you will be your servant. [12] And whoever exalts himself will be humbled, and whoever humbles himself will be exalted (NET).*

22. **Trinity:** a doctrine that describes three persons or entities and is not mentioned in Biblical scriptures. This doctrine was adopted by the self-proclaimed Orthodox church, and after the

Roman Catholic church split out of the Orthodox church, it became one of its biggest proponents. The doctrine was further perpetuated by protestant denominations. The original church that started in Jerusalem by the apostles of the LORD did not teach a Trinity doctrine because they were of a Jewish monotheistic belief system and held to a monotheistic doctrine of one God that stemmed from its Hebrew Shema of Deuteronomy 6:4 Hear, O Israel: The Lord our God is one Lord (KJV).

INDEX OF REFERENCES

Chapter 5

1. Strong, J. (1890). The exhaustive concordance of the Bible: shaliach (Strong's H7975 – one sent)
2. Korteweg, T. (2004). "ORIGIN AND EARLY HISTORY OF THE APOSTOLIC OFFICE". In The Apostolic Age in Patristic Thought. Leiden, The Netherlands: Brill. https://doi.org/10.1163/9789047404293_002 (ed. Hilhorst, p 6f.)

Chapter 6

1. Strong, J. (1890). The exhaustive concordance of the Bible: Elder comes from the Greek word πρεσβύτερος (presbuteros {pres-boo'-ter-os}) which means 1) elder, of age, or 1a) a term of rank or office.
2. Ibid. The exhaustive concordance of the Bible: Greek word ποιμαίνω poimaino {poy-mah'-ee-no} which mean 1) to feed, to tend a flock, keep sheep 1a) to rule, govern or pastor.

Chapter 7

1. Strong, J. (1890). The exhaustive concordance of the Bible: Greek word "οὐρανός ouranos" and is translated as heaven or sky. Its lexical definition is: 1) the vaulted expanse of the sky with all things visible in it 1a) the universe, the world 1b) the aerial heavens or sky, the region where the clouds and the

tempests gather, and where thunder and lightning are produced 1c) the sidereal or starry heavens 2) the region above the sidereal heavens, the seat of order of things eternal and consummately perfect were God dwells and other heavenly beings.

Chapter 9
1. Packer, J. (2000) Telephone Interview by author. (pg. 90)
2. Graham, Billy (1997). Steps to Peace with God (Garland, TX: American Tract Society).
3. Elliff, Jim (1999). Closing with Christ.
4. Ehrhard, J. (1999). The dangers of the invitation system. (pg. 75)

Chapter 10: THE NECESSITY OF WATER BAPTISM
1. Baptism. (1982). In Encyclopedia Britannica (Vol. 1, p. 798).
2. Dana, H. E., & Mantey, J. R. (1949). A Manual Grammar of the Greek New Testament. MacMillan, (pg 104.)
3. New Testament, Greek-English Diglot: (2004). New English Translation, Novum Testamentum Graece (27th ed.). Deutsche Bibelgesellschaft / NET Bible Press. (Note 4, p. 326)
4. Encyclopedia Britannica (1978).
5. Ibid.
6. Howard, G. Hebrew Gospel of Matthew (pg. 151).

7. Beasley-Murray, G. R. (1973). Baptism in the New Testament. Eerdmans. (p. 299).

Chapter 15

1. Brown, F., Driver, S. R., Briggs, C. A., Gesenius, W., & Robinson, E. (1996). The Brown-driver-Briggs Hebrew and English lexicon. In undefined. Hendrickson Publishers.

Chapter 16

1. Hebrew definitions 2. (2021, May 28). Welcome | Precept Austin. https://www.preceptaustin.org/hebrew_definitions_2

Chapter 17

1. Lonergan, Bernard. The Way to Nicea: (1976). The Dialectical Development of Trinitarian Theology. Trans. Conn O'Donovan. Philadelphia: Westminster P. Trans. Of De Deo Trino. Rome: Gregorian UP. 1964. 17-112 (p. 46).
2. Ibid.
3. Ibid.
4. Ibid.
5. Ibid.

6. Zondervan. (2019). NET Bible, full-notes edition, cloth over board, gray, comfort print: Holy Bible. Thomas Nelson. (Col 2:9 Note)

7. 1. Strong, J. (1890). The exhaustive concordance of the Bible:

8. Rimmer, Harry. (1946). The Purposes of Calvary. WM. B. Eerdmans Publishing Company. Grand Rapids, MI. 1946.

9. Rimmer, Harry. (1946). The Purposes of Calvary. WM. B. Eerdmans Publishing Company. Grand Rapids, MI. (p. 13,14)

10. Hooke, S. H. (1963). Babylonian and Assyrian Religion. Norman: U of Oklahoma P. (p. 15-18)

11. Saggs, H. W. F. (1968.) The Greatness that was Babylon: A Sketch of the Ancient Civilization of the Tigris-Euphrates Valley. New York: New American Library.

12. Hislop, Alexander. (1853). The Two Babylons: Or, the Papal Worship. 2nd American ed. Neptune: Loizeaux. 1959.

13. Hart, George. (1990). Egyptian Myths. Austin: U of Texas. (p. 24).

14. Durant, Will. (1935). Our Oriental Heritage. New York: Simon. Vol. 1 of The Story of Civilization. 11 vols. 1935-75. (201)."

15. Hornung, Erik. (1982). Conceptions of God in Ancient Egypt: The One and the Many. Trans. John Baines. Ithaca: Cornell UP. (p. 219).

16. Durant, Will. (1935). Our Oriental Heritage. New York: Simon. Vol. 1 of The Story of Civilization. 11 vols. 1935-75., p. 595.
17. Laing, Gordon Jennings. (1963). Survivals of Roman Religion. New York: Cooper Square Publishers. (p. 128-129.
18. Carter, Jesse Benedict. (1972). The Religious Life of Ancient Rome: A Study in the Development of Religious Consciousness, from the Foundation of the City Until the Death of Gregory the Great. New York: Cooper Square Publishers. (p. 16-19).
19. Ibid., (p. 26)
20. Durant, Will. (1935). Our Oriental Heritage. New York: Simon. Vol. 1 of The Story of Civilization. 11 vols. 1935-75., (p. 595).
21. Laing, Gordon Jennings. Survivals of Roman Religion. New York: Cooper Square Publishers. 1963., p. 130.
22. Rock, T. D. (1867). The mystical woman and the cities of the nations: or, Papal Rome and her secular satellites, by Dionysius. United Kingdom: (pp. 22-23).
23. Najovits, S. R. (2004). Egypt, Trunk of the Tree. United States: Algora Pub.., (pp. 83-84).
24. Graves, Robert (1994). The Larousse Encyclopedia of Mythology. (Sumeria). United Kingdom: Chancellor Press.
25. Sinclair, T. (1991). India. Hong Kong: Odyssey (pp. 382-383).

26. Weigall, A. (2008). The Paganism in Our Christianity. United States: Book Tree., (pp. 197-198).
27. Maurice, T. (1798). The History of Hindostan: Its Arts, and Its Sciences, as Connected with the History of the Other Great Empires of Asia, During the Most Ancient Periods of the World: With Numerous Illustrative Engravings. 2. (1798). - XIX, 372 S.: 7 Ill. United Kingdom: Printed, by H. L. Galabin, for the author; and sold by T. Gardiner., (p. 171).
28. McGiffert, Arthur Cushman. (1932). A History of Christian Thought. Vol. 1. New York: Scribner's. (p. 50).
29. Bauer, Walter. (1979). Orthodoxy and Heresy in Earliest Christianity. Trans. Philadelphia Seminar on Christian Origins. Ed. Robert A. Kraft and Gerhard Krodel. Philadelphia: Fortress. (pp. 56-57).
30. McGiffert, Arthur Cushman. A History of Christian Thought. Vol. 1. New York: Scribner's. 1932. (p. 183)."
31. Ibid. (p. 206)."
32. Campbell, James Marshall. (1963). The Greek Fathers. New York: Cooper Square Publishers. (p. 41).
33. Ibid. (p. 38).
34. Durant, Will. (1935). Our Oriental Heritage. New York: Simon. Vol. 1 of The Story of Civilization. 11 vols. 1935-75. (p. 615).
35. Pelikan, J. (2014). Historical Theology: Continuity and Change in Christian Doctrine. Wipf and Stock Publishers. (p. 22).

36. Lonergan, Bernard. (1976). The Way to Nicea: The Dialectical Development of Trinitarian Theology. Trans. Conn O'Donovan. Philadelphia: Westminster P. Trans. Of De Deo Trino. Rome: Gregorian UP. 1964. 17-112, (p. 56).
37. Ibid. (p. 128).
38. Ibid. (pp. 136-7).
39. Durant, Will. Our Oriental Heritage. (1935). New York: Simon. Vol. 1 of The Story of Civilization. 11 vols. 1935-75. (pp. 342-3).
40. The Soncino Chumash. Ed A. Cohen. 2nd ed. (1983). London: Soncino P. p. 458).
41. Burns, Eugene. (1976). The Doctrine of Christ. np/ Fortman, Edmund J. The Triune God: A Historical Study of the Doctrine of the Trinity. Philadelphia: Westminster P. 1972. / Lonergan, Bernard. The Way to Nicea: The Dialectical Development of Trinitarian Theology. Trans. Conn O'Donovan. Philadelphia: Westminster P. Trans. Of De Deo Trino. Rome: Gregorian UP. 1964. 17-112 (pp. 130).

Chapter 18

1. (See McClintock & Strong 1969, p. 441). (pg. 186)
2. (D'Aubigne 1955, p. 56).
3. Viola, F., & Barna, G. (2010). Pagan Christianity: Exploring the roots of our church practices. Tyndale House Publishers.

4. CHURCH fathers: The Didache. (n.d.). NEW ADVENT. https://www.newadvent.org/fathers/0714.htm
5. Boettner, L. (1962). Roman Catholicism. Presbyterian and Reformed Publishing Co, p 235).

Chapter 19

1. Research guides: Martin Luther as priest, heretic and outlaw: Introduction. (2023, 6). Research Guides at Library of Congress. https://guides.loc.gov/martin-luther-priest-heretic-outlaw/
2. In the July 1980 edition of Abundant Life, Roberts wrote, "Solve your money needs with money seeds" (page 4).

Chapter 21

1. Broderick, R. C., Broderick, V. (1990). The Catholic Encyclopedia. United States: Thomas Nelson.
2. Hayden, M. (2014, December 16). Massachusetts law banning Christmas. Mass.gov. https://www.mass.gov/news/massachusetts-law-banning-christmas#:~:text=In%201659%2C%20the%20Massachu

setts%20Bay,feasting%2C%20or%20any%20other%20way%E2%80%A6

3. Britannica, T. Editors of Encyclopedia (2020, December 6). Does Christmas have pagan roots? Encyclopedia Britannica. https://www.britannica.com/question/Does-Christmas-have-pagan-roots

4. Hillerbrand, H. J. (2024, March 20). Easter. Encyclopedia Britannica. https://www.britannica.com/topic/Easter-holiday

5. Broderick, R. C., Broderick, V. (1990). The Catholic Encyclopedia. United States: Thomas Nelson.
6. Ibid.

About the Author:

James L. Perry Sr. was born and raised in Saginaw, MI to James and Earnestine Perry. He excelled in athletics growing up which provided him an opportunity to play collegiate sports at Central State University and Tuskegee University. After attending a church revival while attending Tuskegee University in Tuskegee, AL at the Apostolic Faith Mission he was converted by the power of GOD. This is where he began preaching and teaching the Gospel of Jesus Christ serving faithfully at the Apostolic Faith Mission as an Associate Minister and in many other ministerial roles. In 2001 he began aiding Bishop George F. Austin in the Louisiana District Council of the PAW, Inc. and was ordained an Elder of the Pentecostal Assemblies of the World, Inc. in August of 2003. Since then, Bro. Perry has evangelized in over twenty of the 50 States and forty cities including Canada. In November 2008 he founded The Church by Christ Jesus in Columbus, Ohio, and pastored for seven years. He is married to the lovely Cynthia Perry and has three beautiful children. Bro. Perry has enjoyed for years the mentorship under the tutelage of Dr. Johnny James (The Walking Bible) who has influenced his ministry greatly and accompanied him in the evangelistic field. Brother Perry's studies include a B.A. in Psychology from Tuskegee University, a B.A. in Pastoral Ministry from Aenon Bible College, a Post Baccalaureate degree in Mental Health Counseling, a Master of Science in Psychology from Grand Canyon University, and is currently finishing a Master of Divinity at Ashland Theological Seminary and a Ph.D. in Integrative Public Policy and Development from Tuskegee University.

For readings and book signings, contact the author at jperryministries@seeksearchstudy.com.

Made in the USA
Columbia, SC
19 May 2025